TWO BIRDS AND NO STONES
It's a short life – fill it!

DEREK AND BERYL HUGHES
'CARTREF'
7 ASH GROVE
NANTWICH
CHESHIRE CW5 7DQ
TEL No. (01270) 623431

"IT'S NOT WHAT YOU'VE DONE..."

"Don't listen to 'em," Uncle Harry would say, "Cram in everything you can, boy. You've not long to fit it all in. It's not what you've done you'll regret, but all the things you've not done! By God! I've done them all!" and he would chortle with recollected pleasure. "Remember, lad, the only sure thing in life is death. Make sure it doesn't beat you!"

TWO BIRDS
AND NO STONES
It's a short life – fill it!

GEOFFREY MORRIS
Illustrated by PATRICIA KELSALL

an imprint of
ANNE LOADER
PUBLICATIONS

ISBN 1 901253 17 1

First published June 2000

Published in Gt Britain by:
Léonie Press
an imprint of
Anne Loader Publications
13 Vale Road
Hartford
Northwich
Cheshire CW8 1PL
Tel: 01606 75660   Fax: 01606 77609
E-mail: anne@aloaderpubs.u-net.com
Websites: http://www.aloaderpubs.u-net.com
http://leoniepress.co.uk

Typeset and printed by:
Anne Loader Publications

About the author and illustrator

Geoffrey Morris was born at Crewe in 1920 and attended Crewe Grammar School before qualifying as a schoolmaster. After volunteering to serve in the Royal Tank Regiment, he left Great Britain with the 50th R.T.R. to join the 8th Army in North Africa. He fought as tank crew from Alamein to Tunis, through Sicily, Italy, Palestine and Greece, was three times wounded and returned to England after  four and a half years of absence. Three days later, by special licence, he married the girl who had waited for him. A school friendship from the age of 10 had developed into a love affair which is still going strong. He taught at Derby, passing through all grades of staffing and retired thankfully in 1980 to settle in France, naturalize and become a French citizen.

He is the author of *Only Fools Drink Water – Forty Years of Fun in Charente-Maritime*, which was entered by the Léonie Press for the Thomas Cook/Daily Telegraph Travel Award 2000.

Patricia Kelsall is a part-time lecturer in Art & Design at Mid-Cheshire College teaching drawing and painting to full-time and part-time students. She has exhibited her work mainly in the North East of England and in Cheshire as well as the Royal Academy in London, the Manchester Academy of Fine Art and at the Annual Salon in Mornant, France – indeed, her work is almost as wellknown in Mornant as it is in Cheshire. Patricia's illustrations and paintings have appeared in numerous publications including Newcastle 900 by Frank Graham, greetings card designs for Bucentaur Gallery and many limited edition publications including publicity brochures, letterheads, menus, local authority town trail leaflets and cast-iron town trail signs. Her paintings have been reviewed in *The Observer Magazine* and *The Guardian* newspaper. She has done almost all the illustrations for the books published by Anne Loader, including *A Bull by the Back Door*, *The Duck with a Dirty Laugh*, *The Way We Were*, *A Nun's Grave*, *Woollyback* and *Only Fools Drink Water* and undertakes many private commissions. She loves doing pictures of France.

Contents

Contents, continued

Photographs

Photographs, continued

DEDICATION

To the memory of Harry whose 'Muck Birds' inspired this book, and to Kathérine Paris who preserved the rough script when the final copy had been lost.

The light-hearted treatment of the 8th Army is in no way derogatory. By inflicting the German Army with its first defeat at Alamein it brought about the beginning of the end. It is just that the author is not a 'muck and bullets' man in spite of receiving his share of both.

Geoffrey Morris

Welcome Little Stranger

My mother, doubtless chuckling heartily from wherever she now rests, was sorely tried throughout her married life. Blessed with one daughter and constantly harassed by the three sons that followed, her life was a very full one. She swung continuously between exasperation and mirth from the toddling stage of the first male child to the marriage of the last.

In later years she was at times heard to remark that the happiest moment of her existence was when she heard the last "I will" uttered by her youngest son and saw him depart to plague a younger woman, as she affectionately put it. Certainly she was always a model mother-in-law. This was due, according to her, to the immense debt of gratitude she owed to her sons' wives for courageously taking them off her hands. The perfect recipe for a harmonious in-law relationship.

Not least of her trials was the anticipated patter of tiny feet intruding into her peace of mind after a blissful gap of nine long

1

years and at the embarrassing age of fifty-two. Thrown at the last fence after a half century of cheerfully surmounting obstacles that would have embittered a lesser woman, she expressed her intentions in unambiguous terms.

Those were not the days of Women's Lib and a quick trip to London when an unpalatable pud was in the oven, but Mother did not, even then, regard her condition with maternal pride and announced her displeasure at my conception with some directness of purpose. Very clearly I was to be no cherished love child.

The carpet on the third step of the stairs became more and more threadbare through her frantic leaps to the hallway each morning. She bought a skipping rope and furiously jumped through the 'hot peppers' of her childhood.

All to no avail. I would not be detached and all she achieved was a degree of athletic fitness remarkable in a woman of her age and condition.

"Just as stubborn then as now," she confided in later years. "I couldn't shake the blighter loose, then or since, until the day of his marriage."

Mother's dry humour finally rendered the situation tolerable and, since the state of affairs was obviously irreversible, due preparations for the more or less happy event were begun.

Baby clothes, perambulator and all the toilet necessities of my elder siblings had gone, optimistically given away or sold long since. I was to rejoice in all things new, albeit with no great glee on Mother's part. Father, on the other hand, was apparently overjoyed, but then he loved children and would not be subdued even by Mother's quite unfair and one-sided attribution of the whole situation to his unseemly carnal appetites.

She went out little as my rapid development became more and more apparent to the casual eye, and attracted the not so casual comments of the local gossips.

Came the long awaited day of her deliverance, and freed at last from the shame and rage at being caught out at her mature age, the mysteries of maternity induced a reluctant pride in the bawling scrap of manhood that she had so tardily produced.

Admiring relatives and friends congratulated her upon the bouncing, bellowing baby, and she began to hold up her head again as she pushed the perambulator on her daily shopping expeditions. It is sad that Fate rarely leaves one undisturbed in mind for very long.

Certainly it need not have decreed that Mother should meet old Mrs Timmis, a farmer's wife and lifelong family friend. Mother proudly pulled down the covers to display my doubtful charms to yet another admiring, envious female. She complacently awaited the time-honoured congratulations; the cooings and ticklings and all the obligatory inanities of the occasion.

Mrs Timmis looked long and hard at me and turned to Mother. Her weather-beaten face crinkled into a smile.

"Eh lass! I'd reyther see a calf onyday," she pronounced.

Secretly my mother was in total agreement with her, and certainly as the years went by, it became increasingly apparent that Mrs Timmis' sense of values was not wholly in error.

My contribution to the population increase of Crewe was to prove no great asset to the town and even less to the immediate vicinity of my birthplace, 60 Ruskin Road.

Bedfast

*M*y earliest recollections of life in our turbulent household revolved around a white kitten, a shantung silk shirt I was made to wear, Harry's pigeons and my own personal fairy who slept all day in my small cot bed. Of all these nebulous recollections the fairy was most real and vivid.

It was a female fairy, slim but quite clearly shaped in the appropriate places, with long narrow gauze-like wings that lay down her back. Quite obviously conceived from some illustration in one of the many books showered upon me by my elder sister; though I am certain that modern trick cyclists would label it earnestly as a classic example of infantile erotic fantasy. They could be right. I thought a lot of my fairy who moved over obligingly when I was put to bed and guarded me against the fearful night fiends that menaced when the light went out.

However, the fairy and I grew and the cot did not, so that at the mature age of three or four, or thereabouts, it was decided that larger sleeping accommodation was required.

My father, a jolly, tubby, kindly man, of whom I shall speak more later, had read the plans for a wooden folding bed. "Capable of supporting in comfort the largest adult, simplicity itself to construct and conveniently small in size, when folded for storage," so said the advertisement.

It was decreed that such a paragon of beds would certainly support my inconsiderable weight and Dad duly sent for the plans and ordered the materials. Now it must be admitted that Father, although a model of virtue in all other respects, was not a born handyman. If he hung a picture the nail fell out, and as for shelving – well, more of that anon.

A trier always, Dad never gave in. He was game for anything. When the plans had been studied and the wood, brackets, hinges and all the other mysteries of wood butchery obtained, he opened his tool box and set to work with an enthusiasm never matched by any of his sons.

He sawed, planed, joined, glued and nailed for the better part of two days. The framework completed, the ends hinged, he tacked on the heavy canvas sheet and stood back to admire his handiwork. Even at this remote distance in time I can recall the pride with which I viewed my bed. For two days I had shadowed Father's every move and now the moment had arrived.

Mother was summoned to share our triumph. Usually her remarks regarding Dad's handicraft efforts verged on the unappreciative if not downright caustic, but this time she was really impressed.

Father, back to the foot of the bed, proudly explained the finer points of the folding procedure to her. Mother, normally rather taciturn by nature, never stinted when praise was truly due.

"Well done, Sam!" she said and thumped him playfully in the chest. Disaster struck. He stepped back, his legs contacted the bed and backwards he fell upon it with a resounding crash.

An ominous splintering sound presaged the end. Slowly and inexorably, rather like a giant clam, the bed closed upon and folded around him. Father disappeared from view and his muffled shouts were certainly never meant for my tender ears.

Mother collapsed as well, tears of mirth rolling down her

cheeks. I was torn between stricken grief at the spectacular disappearance of Father together with all my hopes of a grown-up bed, and convulsive laughter at the struggling heap upon the floor. Mirth prevailed and Mother and I clung to each other in near hysteria.

It was some little time before Dad's increasingly irate bellows induced Mother to prise apart the wreckage and deliver him from the bed's embrace. His first remarks were pithy in the extreme but, as his eyes dwelt upon the debris from which he had risen, his shoulders began to shake a little and a great bellow of laughter came bursting from him. A great man, my Dad.

Only I felt any post jocund sadness at my loss and that rapidly melted away before the promise of a brand new single bed.

I lost out, though. It was a beautiful bed but, somewhere in the transfer, my fairy had flown away. I've never had a fairy in my bed since and, in view of the modern connotation, I don't think I'd like it any more.

Brotherly Love

*V*arious physical scars bear testimony to this day of my somewhat precarious early childhood. They are mainly due to my use, at a tender age, as ballast, passenger, or merely some imaginary character by my elder brother.

Due to the crevasse of years which separated us, I constituted nothing but a profitless nuisance except when I could be utilised on the more hazardous ploys requiring additional weight, a human guinea pig, or just an excuse to be in that particular vicinity.

My most spectacular injuries were acquired during a conscripted Cresta-like run perched on the front end of Harry's trolley. Now, for a clear understanding of this ride, a description of the 'backs' which constituted the course, is essential.

They were 'backs' par excellence: none of your narrow alleyways separating the smaller back to back houses. Our terraced houses once graced the élite of the Victorian railway world and had long gardens in the rear. Between the gardens of the opposing houses was a high walled 'backs' of street width, paved with a ridged pattern to give purchase to the hooves of delivery horses. The 'backs' sloped steadily downhill for a full two hundred yards, interspersed at regular intervals by wide-slotted iron drainage grids.

Harry's trolley, proudly home built, was of ingenious construction worthy of an older hand. A rigidly fixed rear axle carried the smaller wheels of a perambulator, probably recently mine and hopefully pensioned off for good. This was firmly fastened to a very stout cruciform platform of wood on which the rider precariously perched. At the front end the other axle, with large wheels to facilitate the tracking, was fully pivoted by means of a coach bolt and metal plates. Steering was effected by a loop of stout rope, each end of which was fastened to an extremity of the front axle.

Unfortunately, in common with most great constructors, Harry was plagued by teething troubles in his prototype. To steer with any degree of success he was forced to sit far back beyond the rear axle. Here his hefty twelve-year-old weight disturbed the centre of balance to the extent where he repeatedly fell backwards at speed, the front wheels of the trolley reaching for the sky and the back of his head thumping disastrously on the concrete of the 'backs'.

This is where I came in, as a counterpoise. Firmly placed, back resting against his bent legs and thrust well up to the front end, my weight was sufficient to restore the equilibrium.

To the accompaniment of my very vocal objections we set off. The position was not without interest. Ridged concrete hurtled beneath my startled gaze at incredible speed and proximity. Vibration from those same ridges shimmered the vision, chattering teeth and bones, an effect greatly accentuated by the absence of tyres which had long since been shaken apart and torn from the steel rims by the brutal shuddering.

No harm befell until the first grid hove in sight. Harry pulled on the steering gear. The left wheel inclined inwards, the naked rim carving the outer side of my knee with the efficiency of a buzz saw. I was oblivious. Mixed terror and relief at evading the grid

8

constituted a very effective anaesthetic.

Each time we approached the pitfall of a grid, the front wheels, responding to Harry's frantic heaves to left or right, veered in from one side or the other and, until I acquired the necessary defensive agility, the tyreless rims sliced me unmercifully.

There was no way I could win. Not a hope of descent at that speed and Harry's designs had never included brakes. When droplets of blood in the slipstream acquainted him with what was happening up forward he ceased to steer and down into the wide slots of a grid dropped one of the offending wheels. The dramatic deceleration catapulted me from the trolley as from an ejector seat and I was airborne for what seemed an age before my head made forcible contact with the concrete.

Reassured by the strength of my howling protests that the blood on my head did not constitute a risk to my continued existence, Harry replaced me in the seat of honour and we rolled on again, this time towards home and plasters.

The grid I fear had done nothing to improve the vehicle's tracking and, once at speed, no effort on Harry's part would divert the trolley from its self-chosen course. Inevitably and inexorably we headed for the wall, eyes tightly closed. On impact I formed a very effective cushion and Harry escaped unscathed. I was never held in high esteem by my elder brothers but at times like these I had my uses.

Harry led me home, hair and socks full of blood, skin missing from chin and nose, everywhere liberally besmirched with oil and dirt. Relief at no longer hurtling about my little universe brought such comfort that I ceased to blubber.

"Remember," said Harry in an elder brother voice, "you fell down. Didn't you?"

He was ever an optimist. Before I could get out a word Mother seized Harry by the collar and shook him.

"You've had him on that trolley," she said, in a voice almost impassioned for her. "I'm going to skelp you, my lad!" And she did. I winced for him even more than I did later whilst she dressed my injuries.

In retrospect I think she was a little hard on Harry. After all, at three months I had fallen head first out of my pram. At twelve months Dad had bounced me joyfully up and down upon his shoulder whilst heedlessly walking beneath the stone lintel of our back gate. I bear the scars of that one still. About the age of four I fell over my own pile of bricks, landed on my chin and almost completely severed my protruding tongue. It was sewed back successfully and life went on.

In early Junior School the head of a workman's hammer detached and flew across the classroom on a pre-destined trajectory. When an apprehensive teacher took me home, bloodstained and bandaged about the head, my mother greeted him with: "What's he done this time? Hand him over!"

At Grammar School, the ancient wiring of a classroom ceiling rose short-circuited and burned through, dropping the heavy porcelain shade and bulb directly upon my skull where it shattered into fragments. Quite unjustly the teacher who had switched on the lights regarded me with suspicion rather than compassion. She still had memories of my elder brother.

In this same class suspicion one again unjustly fell upon me. We were still in the gloom of 'Means Test' days and, although all of us in that particular group held the County Scholarship, those whose parents had the means were obliged to buy all their own textbooks.

This state of affairs certainly educated me into a keen knowledge of buying and selling. We sold and bought at half and quarter price any relevant books to or from our immediate junior and senior co-pupils. Outside sources were not neglected either and I was delighted to obtain my copies of Shakespeare at sixpence a pocket volume from Woolworths.

All went well until the first class reading with parts duly allotted. Boldly I proclaimed my piece: "The bawdy hand of the dial is now upon the prick of noon!"

There was a pregnant hush, then the girls began to titter. This stimulated the lads into a roar of unseemly laughter and Mr Hodgkinson into a bellow of: "Bring your text here, Morris!"

Once again the Morris lack of foresight had led me to ignore the flysheet of my copy, on which was clearly printed: "Full, unexpurgated edition." Everyone else possessed the carefully emasculated version suited to our tender years. The flysheet saved me from retribution, but when we resumed our reading and the quotation "Here comes Mercutio without his roe, like a dried herring" fell from my lips, Old Hodge could no longer contain himself.

"Only a Morris could do it twice," he roared. "You *are* the last, aren't you?"

So, Harry's trolley had just been one more incident in the obviously preselected pattern, and indeed my Mother was often heard to observe feelingly that the repeated impacts suffered by my head might well account for a very great deal.

The Iron Bridge

N one of the family was ever content to stay in one place for
very long and the urge of wanderlust set in at an unusually
early age in all of the boys.

My mother often spoke of the frantic anxiety she experienced
during the prolonged absences of Frank, the eldest. By the time
Harry came along, this was reduced to mere curiosity and a dispassionately tanned backside for the wanderer, in an effort to dis-
courage him from the error of his ways. When I made my belated
appearance upon the Morris scene, even the curiosity had then
given way to a philosophical acceptance and the punishment
reduced to a mere formality; a kind of obligatory ritual that must
be undertaken to fulfil parental responsibility.

Of us all my mother said: "You can't lose them. They all turn up
like bad pennies." Many years later, during wartime, she had no
worries on account of her uniformed sons, two of them flying and
the youngest in a tank regiment, all overseas on active service.
"It'll take more than a war to cope with that lot," she said. "It's the

rest I feel sorry for!"

Even when Frank's aircraft was missing and she received a War Office telegram informing her that I was severely wounded and on the danger list she remained unperturbed.

"They'll be all right," she said. And they were. Back they came, in due course, after years of dodging hurtful missiles, to be told: "Wipe your feet and come in. Your tea's ready."

My absences began at the unusually mature age of five. By the state of my foot gear Mother knew that considerable distances had been covered. At that time the roads were almost free from traffic, and child molesters must have been much fewer. In any case, to quote Mother: "The devil looks after his own."

As long as I wandered off by myself all was well, I would return in due time. Unfortunately I had a mate. A delicately nurtured little boy who was dear to me on account of his uncle who allowed us to ride behind the horse drawing his coal cart. I can still experience in my mind the ecstasy of jogging down the 'backs' behind that magnificent rump and swishing tail. And when the horse broke wind! But I must not digress in reminiscences.

Neville Slack, as he was called, would not normally have left the clearly delineated territory of our 'backs' at any price. What made him accompany me I no longer recall, but off we set, Neville in his immaculate little suit and fragile shoes contrasting oddly with my burly jersey and tiny hob-nailed boots.

We followed my favourite route, down the length of the 'backs', onto the main road and down through the centre of town. It was a railway town, and away on the far side of it was a fascinating junction of myriads of lines, all converging on the loco sheds and engineering works. These lines bisected this quarter of the town, and loftily spanning them was a massive iron footbridge dating from before the turn of the century.

It was a wonderful place. Fully a hundred yards of box-like sheet iron tunnel, open only to the sky. The sides were high, but irresistibly intriguing rusted holes gave distorted Olympian views of the activities of lesser mortals below. It echoed and clanged to even our light footfalls, and the access steps at either end seemed innumerable. Height and view gave a god-like feeling of detachment from the confines of a small child's circumscribed environment. In a word, it was heaven.

Neville and I scaled the ringing steps and clattered our way along to my favourite rust hole. Pressing eager eyes to the jagged spy hole and our bodies to the iron walls, we spied upon the lesser beings below.

It was not till we pulled away to excitedly discuss our observations that the awful disaster became apparent. Since my last visit to the beloved bridge, the maintenance crew had passed that way leaving a glutinous heavy coat of tar upon the whole of the iron work. Faces, hands and the front of all our apparel were liberally besmirched with glistening black that stretched like chewing gum as we vainly plucked at it.

Reasonably philosophical because of past experience, I was prepared to suffer the inexplicable adult disapproval of such accidents, but not so Neville.

He rubbed his hands pathetically down his once neat suit, threw back his head and howled. The tears flowed down his blackened face without even furrowing the tar. I threw my arms around him in an effort to comfort him and thereby ensured that he was coated in the rear as well as the front.

It was not easy piloting the blubbering Neville along the three or so miles back home, but that was nothing compared to the trials to come.

Mrs Slack, in near hysterics, had been far from calmed by Mother's casual advice to wait a bit till they came home. Neighbourly relations were stretched to breaking point when we hove in sight.

With a shriek of relief, Mrs Slack clasped her long lost offspring to her bosom and planted a hefty kiss upon his face. Mother, with greater experience in such matters, seized me by the ear and held me at arm's length.

Mrs Slack had just released Neville from her close embrace and stood up, blackened well in face and bosom, when my Father returned from work. With true Morris tact, he called across, "What? Have you all joined the Black Minstrels, then?"

Relations were never the same again. Neville and I met sometimes on the sly, but my expeditions to the Iron Bridge were always solitary from then until my courting days.

The Weaker Sex?

*O*ur small pre-school gang did not actively despise girls. It was just that they were of no great use in our scheme of things. They could not fight very well, cried if their clothes were torn and generally disliked any activity which made them dirty or dishevelled. Since all worthwhile pastimes took place in gloriously filthy environments, this made them a great liability. Indeed we could never understand why our elder brothers were forever hanging around their female contemporaries and even cajoling them to pair off for seemingly pointless expeditions to quiet places away from the others. All very mysterious.

However we were not bigoted. There were one or two more enlightened small girls of our age who did not mind soiling their hands and clothes and actually enjoyed a good rough and tumble. These we admitted to our gang. As second-rate members be it understood, but none the less, members.

But for these superior few we should have reached school age as confirmed misogynists, steady bachelors for life. The other girls were the bane of our existence. Should we return from some memorable foray covered with mud or soaked in water, one or other of our members' sisters would see to it that our parents were fully informed of all the relevant circumstances. MI5 or the German SS intelligence could have learned much from the sisterly spy system.

Just a few remained strictly neutral; they neither joined in with us nor did they 'shop' us. Mostly these girls had no brothers of their own. One such girl was Maggie Fiddler, a very dainty self-possessed little being who ignored us as we did her. She looked very fragile and was easily frightened by any physical danger, but we never took advantage of this because any knowledge of our activities that Maggie acquired stayed with her. She never informed the adult world in order to amass credit in high places. We respected this.

As a gang we were fearless. Individually we might be afraid of the dark at night or of Old Man Bailey and his wire haired terrier, but together we ruled our small world. We built dens, frequented one another's cellars, knocked on doors and ran away. Intrepid we were and often quite deviously intelligent in our constant battle against the adult world on whom we so depended after sunset.

Old Ma Green hated us all. Not just for what we did. We felt she disliked us for what we were. I suppose now that she did. Poor old soul, she was at the end of the road and all alone; we were at the very start and still in the herd.

Her fury when we knocked on her door and fled was a constant joy to us. She would rush out into her front garden, waving her fist and calling maledictions upon us. Heartlessly we fell about in innocent thoughtless laughter.

One day we had a touch of inspiration. Jimmy Bowey borrowed a long stout cord from his father's shed. Stealthily we crept into Ma Green's front garden, tied one end to her front door knob, stretched the rope tightly to the front gate and secured it there. The doors were now firmly linked.

Jimmy was given the honour of knocking on the door. He fled, leaving open the front gate. Out came Ma Green, shaking her fist to the sky. She spotted the open front gate, scuttled to it and angrily swung it closed.

Too late she heard the front door slam shut behind her under the pull of Jimmy's rope. Faced with a hundred yards tramp round the terrace to reach her back door she looked dismayed and we eagerly anticipated an unsurpassed burst of rage. At a safe distance we stood transfixed as Ma Green looked first at the gate, then at the door, spotted the rope and burst into peal after peal of hearty laughter. It was the first time we had ever seen her smile.

"Come here!" she shouted, wiping her eyes. "Come here the lot of you!"

Cautiously we approached, mindful from past experience of the perfidy of which adults were capable.

She was still laughing when we stood sheepishly in front of her.

"I've never laughed so much since my husband slipped on the tripe," she said. "Come round with me. I've got a sweetie or two tucked away somewhere."

Ma Green became our firm friend, one of the gang almost, an honorary member, anyway. She loved to have us playing about in her back yard. We loved the odd cake and sweet that frequently came our way and, glowing with self-righteousness, importantly did her minor local shopping for her.

She proved a tower of strength and reassurance when our private nightmare, the nemesis of school, engulfed us one by one. I was the youngest, consequently the last to go, and parental platitudes and the comforting words of Old Ma Green did little to dispel the gloom of impending incarceration.

Maggie Fiddler started school on the same day as myself and it was Maggie's mother who took us both together. Maggie trotted ahead in eagerness to arrive and I trailed miserably behind, hand firmly grasped by Mrs Fiddler.

Brave of face and quivering like a jelly inside, I took my place in class next to timid little Maggie.

My stolid pose remained intact until Miss Lockley cast her spectacled glance around the class. The light reflected fearsomely from those glasses as they came to rest on me.

"You are Geoff, aren't you?" she asked.

"Yes, Miss," I blurted, and burst into floods of tears.

Maggie threw her arms round me and hugged.

"It's all right," she said. "School's lovely!"

I sniffed three or four times and dried my eyes on her hanky.

How were the mighty fallen!

Maggie's enthusiasm lasted throughout her life in Infant, Junior, Grammar Schools and University, to culminate in the headship of a large Grammar School from which she has long since retired. A truly round peg in a circular hole, Margaret Fiddler was one of the few thoroughly stabilised enthusiasts of this world.

'Old Scrooge'

*E*arly school life always lacked the clarity of purpose, stability of beliefs and the vivid sensations experienced during pre-school freedom. These qualities only returned later when the onset of puberty in a mixed grammar school put fire into our veins. Consequently this interim period emerges only as isolated impressions and incidents which had little bearing on the declared purpose of education.

Our new world was governed by many masters. The one for whom I had most regard was Old Scrooge. He was not aged by any means, everyone in those days above the doddering age of twenty-five was 'Old' to us. His real name escapes me now, so Scrooge he must remain, a nickname earned by his remarkable performance in a staff production of Dickens' "A Christmas Carol".

He was a hard man, never smiling in class and with a ready cane for those transgressions disturbing law and order. It was no token swish that we received. When that cane came down across the fingers the eyes watered in sympathy. Many were the beliefs that peculiar practices could alleviate the distress; a surreptitious licking of the hand prior to punishment, a hair plucked from the head and laid across the palm, a carefully timed lowering of the hand as the cane struck. None had the slightest effect except the latter which ensured that contact was made excruciatingly at the very tips of the fingers.

Very painful, but all of us preferred Old Scrooge's summary punishment to the tongue lashings of other teachers. Once the cane had descended the slate was wiped clean and relations instantly restored; no grudges, no favourites.

Over and done with on the spot.

I must have suffered an average number of Scrooge's licks, as we called them, but at this distance I recall but two occasions. One happened during an art lesson. The class was busily engaged in drawing various misshapen versions of a vase of daffodils, all except me. Painstakingly I was drawing and embellishing a head and shoulders portrait of Old Scrooge. It did not flatter him, and in the middle of pencilling in a few warts I sensed a presence behind me. I looked up straight into the eyes of Scrooge himself.

Shock must have scrambled my senses a little, because, just for an instant, I could have sworn he was grinning. One blink and the normal stern image returned. A hand reached over my shoulder and seized the paper.

"Out, boy!"

Left hand tightly thrust beneath the armpit in the time honoured cure, I resumed a one-handed attack on the daffodils.

Obviously it was a day of mild hallucinations because, at play time, unseemly bursts of mirth issued from the open staff room door. Peeping cautiously in, I could see Old Scrooge displaying something to his colleagues. Had I not known better I could have sworn that it was my portrait, except, of course, it was unthinkable that such sacrilege could provoke merriment among the mighty.

Not even the sneakiest amongst us held much brief for Smarmy, a diligently well-mannered teacher beloved of the less discerning parents. Never at a loss for words, he talked incessantly, conveying nothing. Towards us he was gentleness itself, full of soft words and exhortations; a veritable kindly pedagogue whose avuncular approaches made us squirm and whom we instinctively disliked. Occasionally his loss of self-control revealed a little of the inner man and we liked this still less. He taught us little simply because he knew little himself but, a true educational 'con' man, he talked himself into a headship long before I left the school. Times change little. The Smarmies are still with us!

Harding, so unexceptional that he did not merit a nickname, was, I now realise, a progressive, an avant garde teacher. His methods were spectacular and new, marvellous to see and teaching very little. Having ruined all our early maths, he passed on to higher things, wafted up on the wings of his wonderful modern methods.

The remaining staff were honest nonentities, teaching and controlling us more or less efficiently. They had a thankless task. We owed them much and Scrooge more. The latter left his signature upon our outstretched palms along with a valuable legacy of steadiness and a belief in justice.

He once intervened in a memorable fight I had with Freddy Tucker. Tucker, an unusually burly lad with a perpetually running nose, had plagued our lives by his bullying from the age of seven. I had suffered unmercifully at his hands simply, I think, by reason of an inherent antipathy which I was too guileless to conceal.

Around nine years of age it slowly dawned on me that I had grown proportionately faster than my tormentor and I was no longer inferior in size. The result of this conclusion was inevitable.

Tucker picked on me as we left school. Surrounded by a mob of blood-lusting schoolmates, we commenced to batter one another. Comparable now in size and strength, I had the incomparable advantage of two years' solid persecution and hate.

Looking back, I feel some shame at the thrashing meted out to Tucker. Repeatedly he attempted to break and run and equally repeatedly he was thrown back by his former victims now surrounding us. Bleeding profusely, battered and tearful, he must have heard Scrooge's bellow as the trumpets of salvation.

Scrooge's face had been visible at the staffroom window throughout the combat, and, as he led us off cane-wards, I vaguely wondered why he had not dashed out, as was his normal habit, to end the strife at its onset.

He whacked us both of course, Tucker first with a fearsome swish which made me blench in anticipation. I hardly felt mine, a fact which puzzled me no end.

Had it not been wholly unimaginable I could have believed a smile and wink accompanied the stroke he dealt me.

Bowey's Ghost

As lads we were very lucky compared to the modern youth. We had no youth clubs, no play areas, no ready-made facilities, no television and no public pre-occupation with our welfare. Consequently we had to think for ourselves and provide our own entertainments which were far richer in experience and more satisfying than the canned, preserved and recycled amusements titty-sucked by the majority of the poor pampered kids today. They miss a lot. Small wonder they protest.

Even as small boys we had our broad 'backs', the various cellars of our terraced houses for wet days and our own gangs for expeditions which were too full of imaginative purpose to require any needless destruction or vandalism to turn us on. We organised our own pastimes, not perhaps with the polish of a modern youth club, but we enjoyed ourselves immensely and harmed no-one very much.

The cellars were our greatest asset in the British climate. A sure refuge on wet days and a haven of security from adult interference. Bowey's cellar was especially fine. It had mice, lots of them. When tired of fighting or play acting and with all the worthwhile boasting done, there always remained a mouse hunt. We never actually caught any but the excitement of the chase and the planning of new strategy never palled. Most of our inconsiderate parents used their cellars for storage purposes and trapped the mice. Bowey's cellar, uncluttered and mousey, remained the supreme attraction until the Wrights moved into Ruskin Road.

Wright was a natural for our mob. Handy with his fists, goodnatured and generous with the toffees, he superseded Bowey from the first time we entered his cellar.

On tip-toe, in dead silence at Wrighty's insistence, we installed ourselves. It was not much of a cellar to look at; rather like our own, full of junk and not a mouse to be seen. But then, as we looked round in disappointment, the entertainment began.

A loud groan came from the room above, several mysterious knocks and a sepulchral query, "Is there anybody there? Rap twice for 'yes'. Is there anybody there?"

Wrighty's mother, a leading light in the local spiritualist group, was holding a *séance* with the other old biddies of the district.

We hugged ourselves in silent mirth as the rappings and whispers continued. Wrighty's superior grin grew wider. No-one could match this for wet-day entertainment. Unable to contain ourselves in silence any longer, we hastily adjourned to Bowey's cellar for a long and rowdy discussion on procedure for the next week's *séance*. Even the mice were forgotten.

During the following week a strange assortment of apparatus gradually accumulated in Bowey's cellar. There was a long broom handle, a hand bell, two or three cardboard tubes and some stiff paper that crackled loudly when roughly handled.

Séance day came round and armed with these impedimenta, we crept down Wrighty's cellar in dead silence and waited. Footfalls above, followed by the scraping of chair and table legs announced the arrival of the good ladies in Mrs Wright's parlour. The swish of drawn curtains and the protesting creaks as weighty bottoms lowered onto the circle of chairs told us that communication with the spirits was about to begin.

We listened in silence through the preliminary rappings and mutterings. Then, when we felt the atmosphere was established, Bowey took the initiative. Broom handle held high above his head, he responded to a tap of inquiry with a fusillade of raps on the ceiling of the cellar.

A dead silence followed this spiritual response. Then came a quavering query:

"Is there anybody there? Do you wish to speak with anyone here?"

Oliver groaned lugubriously down his cardboard tube and Alf tinkled his handbell gently. More raps came from above and below before the meeting over our heads broke up in alarm at Oliver's plaintive moans. What they thought he was we never knew. He sounded to us more like a cow in labour than an ethereal spirit.

We sat very quietly till the coast was clear before giving vent to our laughter. At the height of "Did you hear this? Did you hear them hurry out?", Bowey lifted his broom handle and dramatically re-enacted his rappings for our greater enjoyment, adding for good measure:

"Is there anybody there? Rap to communicate."

The grins froze on our faces as several hard raps came back through the solid cellar wall. We stood stock still as a ghostly slithering sound, followed by a muffled clanking, repeated itself several times. A final clank sped us up the steps and out into daylight like greased lightning.

Even after we learned of how Ma Newton, the Wright's next door neighbour, had chosen so unfortunate a moment to hammer her coal to a convenient size and shovel it into her bucket, there remained some amongst us very reluctant to enter that cellar again. Bowey's mouse-ridden cellar, an unghostly underworld, once more reigned supreme.

The Helping Hand

As long as I could remember, which was not so long at that stage, the parlour chimney had never been swept. The parlour was not a room we often used, except on Sundays, high days, holidays and perhaps for receiving the occasional visitor whom we did not know intimately. Consequently, the fire was not lit frequently and no-one bothered very much about the odd tiny wisp of smoke that drifted back into the room instead of going chimneywards.

It was during the visit of Aunt Alice from Preston that the crisis arose.

The wisps became puffs, the puffs developed into clouds and by the second day the smoke in the room had become intolerable. Aunt Alice, always forthright, announced that the chimney must be swept.

Now this presented us with a problem. Since the local sweep's efforts at clearing the kitchen chimney, diplomatic relations between Mother and him had been irrevocably severed. She had described his methods and the mess he made in terms normally reserved for her sons. Not unnaturally he took exception to this and departed without even demanding payment for work done.

Undaunted, the entire household rallied round with innumerable suggestions. Father's offer to borrow rods and do the job himself were met with an emphatic refusal. This was not unjustified ingratitude since, through no apparent fault of his own, almost all his handiwork attempts ended in disaster.

Frank and Harry had their own plans, which varied from inserting me, in the role of chimney sweep boy complete with handbrush, to pulling through the chimney from the rooftop with the aid of a small shrub tied onto a stout rope. Both Mother and I stamped on the first suggestion. One could never be quite sure in our house whether or not such ideas were facetious. She vetoed the last because of the trouble involved should Frank or Harry fall from the steeply pitched roof of our tall terraced house. As usual, they were full of other ingenious ideas, all rejected by Mother as even 'dafter' than stuffing me up the chimney, 'Water Babies' fashion.

It was at this point of stalemate that we had a visit from Uncle Harry who lived at no great distance but whom we seldom saw in our house. Probably he only came to provoke and enjoy a spirited argument with Aunt Alice, thereby ensuring a healthy continuation of their mutual antipathy.

Uncle Harry, although in retirement, was a shooting and fishing man and his approach to all problems was a little cavalier, a characteristic inherited, according to Mother, from her own somewhat eccentric father.

"There's no problem here," announced Uncle Harry brusquely, "I don't know why you're all standing around with faces like Liverpool Orange Men at a Catholic Wakes. I'll come back tomorrow and clear that lot for you!"

He departed, omitting his usual altercation with Aunt Alice. An omen like that should have aroused some misgivings, that and the uncharacteristic eagerness to assist his relatives, all of whom shunned him a little as the family reprobate.

True to his word, early next morning, Uncle Harry reappeared complete with his chimney cleaning equipment, a double-barrelled twelve bore and a handful of number six cartridges. He took forceful charge of the operation.

"Put a sheet over the fireplace and leave a hole for me to work through," he said. Mother suggested that a few precautions should be taken. Covers for the carpet and easy chairs perhaps? The pictures and ornaments removed? Uncle Harry dismissed such trivialities contemptuously.

"No need for that. I'm not going to ram a dirty brush up and down like a fiddler's elbow. Just stand well back!"

So saying, he inserted the gun through the gap in the sheet, thrust it high into the offending chimney and pulled both triggers.

We expected a bang, but the explosion and reverberation in the chimney stunned us all. The sheet flew from the fireplace and across the room as though on wings of its own. There came an almighty rumbling from the chimney and the soot, accompanied by an odd brick end or two, descended.

The empty grate filled with a peculiarly fluffy-sounding thump and soot billowed out across the parlour in a dense all pervading cloud. We fled, Uncle Harry close on our heels. Choking and coughing in the back yard, we took stock of each other. Uncle Harry, who had received the full force of the descent, was blacker than any negro minstrel. His false teeth and red-veined eyes gleamed unnaturally white through the coat of soot, more of which rose in clouds from his clothes as he tentatively patted them. It was the first and last time I ever saw him lost for words.

The rest of us had nothing to laugh about. We'd all received our fair share. Mother led us silently back to the parlour door. Soot lay everywhere. Piled high in the fireplace, it spilled wide out across the carpet and lay in a thick black coating over furniture and curtains. Indeed, the continuing fallout from the floating black cloud was still considerable.

Mother gently shut the door and turned to Uncle Harry. She spoke at some length and in terms my innocent ears had never heard from her lips before. Uncle Harry, the incorrigible, had met his Waterloo; though it must be said on his behalf that speech and thought must have been difficult to project through the amount of soot that coated his face and choked his lungs.

Anyway, it was again the first and last time anyone ever saw Uncle Harry turn his hand to domestic chores of any sort. As Mother said afterwards, it was almost worth the mess to see him brushing away on hands and knees. Not that the rest of us werei̇dle. All day it took to restore some semblance of order.

Finally, when the fire was lit and drawing merrily, Uncle Harry began, "At least it..."

He encountered Mother's eye and got no further.

It was a week of mishaps, starting badly when I dropped a jar of frog spawn in the yard and decided to cut my losses by making an out of season slide upon it. No harm might have ensued had I remembered to clear it up afterwards, or even had Mrs Walker, our somewhat voluble neighbour, not chosen to call round. Her shriek as she slipped and sat in it echoed through the neighbourhood, telling me very clearly that retribution was nigh. It was, and it overtook me within the hour.

This minor incident preceded the chimney episode, after which the atmosphere or, perhaps to use a much more expressive French word, the 'ambience' of the Morris household was not all it could be. The tension tended to repercuss adversely on our least infringements of decorum and Harry enlisted my help to embark on a conciliatory course of helpfulness.

Now, Father was a very keen and competent rose grower. He developed and grafted his own stock which was locally renowned. In size, shade and scent his roses were universally acclaimed throughout a district where everyone prided himself as a rose grower.

This was long before the days of packaged fertiliser to suit the individual needs of every garden plant. True fanciers all had their own recipes to promote growth and flowering.

Father pinned his faith, with some justification, on marinated pig manure. He had a large barrel filled with water into which every week he vigorously stirred half a bucket of pig muck. When the noxious mixture had settled and matured, the clear noisome yellow liquid was carefully applied to the roots of each rose bush with a large syringe. This took some time to do and ate into the limited periods he was at home.

Harry's idea was that we should each take a syringe and a

bucket of the pungent elixir and conscientiously manure the roses, thereby saving Father's time when he was next off duty and gaining credit for the future. Full of conscious virtue, we applied the potion, as directed, to bush after bush.

All would have been well had not I backed into a particularly thorny variety and, in reflex leap, discharged my syringe skywards.

Harry thoughtfully wiped the pig muck from his hair, carefully filled his syringe and shot the contents into my grinning face. This was too much even for small fry and for five or ten minutes, until the buckets were empty, a twin barrage of pig muck shot from opposing sides of the garden. Ammunition exhausted, we stood dripping gently, the enormity of the situation slowly conquering mirth.

We squelched up to the back door with a vague idea of cleaning up before nemesis overtook us. The door opened as we stood there. Mother recoiled a step, wrinkling her nose as the odour preceded us.

"Stay there!" she commanded. 'In the middle of the yard!"

The end of a hose was thrown from the doorway and water spurted. Mother emerged, picked up the hose and directed the stream upon us. We howled as the cold water hit us under pressure, but this was not all. The last of the pig muck swilled from our garments, Mother demanded:

"Strip and drop your clothes in the bowl here."

We did and once more received a bashing from the water as Mother unmercifully hosed us down.

"Get inside and run a hot bath," she ordered, turning off the water.

Thankfully we dashed upstairs and even more thankfully we heard Mother's paroxysms of laughter from down below. Saved by her sense of humour, we slid into the bath. It had been some week!

The Old Block and All That

My maternal grandfather, whom I never saw, had been a millwright. Mother was the youngest of a large family, I was a very belated addition to her children, and consequently the generation gap between grandfather and myself was vast. In fact our dates of birth were over a century apart.

This was something I greatly regretted, for, listening to Mother's accounts of him, he emerged as a consultant millwright of such repute that, in the new age of industry developing at a phenomenal rate, his services entailed travelling countrywide. He was, in fact, a last century trouble shooter.

Mother's descriptions were so vivid that I felt I knew the man. He travelled as a gentleman and, to do the job for which he had been summoned, he would change into snow-white corduroy overalls to distinguish him from the drably clad workmen he directed.

Although Mother spoke with some pride of his engineering

reputation, she was vaguely ashamed of some aspects of her father's beliefs. He was obviously an eccentric. In an age when it was unmanly not to smoke, he would do so, with an expression of great distaste, in order to prove his manhood and, immediately afterwards, wash out his mouth and gargle with water to clear away the taste. Almost with horror, Mother spoke of his outspoken atheism in an age when this was most unseemly.

"What has Jimmy Jesus ever done for me?" he would ask when his daughters gently remonstrated with him. "Can he weld on new cogs or set up an epicyclic gear?"

He seldom drank but when he did it was on an heroic scale distressful to his staid and respectable family. Altogether a non-conformer in an age of strict conformity, his reaction to any situation was unpredictable. I do not know how he lived during his long working absences from home and this is a matter of great regret.

The poor man received the blame for all our escapades.

"It's your Grandfather coming out," Mother would say to us, "You'll end up like your Uncle Harry!"

This dire threat never seemed very frightening to us. Uncle Harry, the family black sheep, had also been a clever engineer and was living out a luxurious retirement in much better circumstances than the rest of us.

Mother was right of course, enough of the turbulent blood had come down to us to stir up the household occasionally but, with it, we also inherited a fair degree of his ability to make and tame mechanical things. The combination, though sometimes not a happy one, gave us sound interests outside of the academic lives we were destined to follow.

Because of this our early toys were all mechanical, the serious building type, or else sets of real tools, not the toy mockeries usually foisted upon the young.

An early construction set given to me rejoiced in the unlikely name of 'Cliptico', I suppose because the tubes etc. clipped together without benefit of bolts.

I became very adept in making original pieces of workable nonsense that variously afflicted the household with noise, draughts and occasional injuries.

My *piece de résistance*, without a doubt, was the Sand Mill.

A huge wheel was pivoted on upright supports rather like the old Big Wheel at Blackpool. It carried little hoppers or buckets round its circumference and, poised above, there was a large container shaped in the form of a hollow inverted pyramid with a small hole at the apex.

My design was good. Sand was to fill the container, pour through the hole onto the hoppers, and drive round the wheel. No prototype is ever perfect, of course, and there was no provision to catch the falling sand when its task was concluded.

I was justifiably proud of this and, the instant it was completed, I departed on an urgent sand hunt. There were new houses under construction at no great distance and I headed confidently in that direction. To my chagrin, the builders had reached a stage of construction where sand was no longer being used. I wandered disconsolately inside one of the houses.

The walls were in process of plastering and raw plaster of Paris lay around in abundance. Happily I scooped the powdery stuff into the end of an old cement bag, liberally whitening myself in the act, and, bag slung over shoulder, departed gleefully homewards.

The cement bag, not in the first flush of youth, released a fair quantity of plaster down my back during the journey and laid quite a trail over the step into the kitchen where I lugged it across the floor to the Sand Mill.

Reservoir hopper well filled with plaster dust, I took my finger cautiously from the feed hole and released the flow. It was spectacular. Plaster poured briskly down and, as the wheel gained momentum, the hoppers whirled round flinging the dust far and wide like sparks from a catherine wheel.

Light enough to float about in the air, what was not hurled en masse round the table, floor and cupboards, settled slowly in a fine coating over everything in sight. The kitchen grew hazy and it was not until I began to cough and choke that some of the glamour of success subsided enough for me to appreciate the gravity of the situation. Action was needed, and quickly, before Mother's return.

My hand was on the brush when she crossed the threshold. Normally never at a loss for words to fit a situation, she stood transfixed, looking round the kitchen as though doubting the veracity of her vision. Still wordless, she strode across to the briskly revolving mill, seized it with both hands and hurled it into the yard, She followed it out and literally war danced upon it, still in ominous silence.

Breathlessly, she turned towards me. Only my stricken face at the sight of the mangled wreckage saved me.

"Get it all cleared up," she said in quiet menace. "Start dusting at the top and work down to the floor. If there's a speck left when I come back..."

She left; to regain control, I think.

Two hours it took me to restore some degree of order to the kitchen and all the while my shattered Cliptico lay in sight. An odd tear or two furrowed my powdered cheeks. I'd been very fond of it.

Mother said nothing more when she returned with a parcel under her arm. She still said nothing when I opened it at breakfast next day. She was fair, my mother, hard but fair. It was a brand new Cliptico.

The 'Muck Birds' & Other Fancies

Three sons were not the only living things that, from time to time, disturbed the even tenor of the household. We were apt to take an interest in the more unusual of animals that came our way and, even on the occasions when our choice fell on perfectly ordinary and mundane creatures to keep, they seemed to acquire something of the attitude and unfortunate panache of their owners.

It would take too long to describe in detail the complete sequence of events resulting from the normally steady, respectable, hobby of pigeon keeping taken up by my elder brothers. All the same, a brief account of the way in which such an activity always escalated into a household crisis will help to explain why my own little pets were seldom welcomed.

My mother, by now sadly cynical and experienced in all matters relating to her sons, should have known better than to encourage an interest in the 'fancy'. So calm a pastime, she thought, would be good for them. It would give them a sense of responsibility and surely be devoid of all possibility of any repercussions to involve her incident prone family.

The pigeons prospered. They fed well and, in the normal process of such matters, left their marks abundantly and with increasing frequency upon Mother's washing. They by no means confined their natural functions to our own back yard. The neighbours, too, received their fair due and before long the pigeons were heard to be uncharitably referred to as the 'Morris Muck Birds', an endearment with which Mother heartily concurred.

Like their owners, the pigeons were never half hearted about their projects. They bred. Prolifically. Before long, when the loft door was opened, the sky darkened and the flapping of wings was awe inspiring. Quite Biblical in some ways but for the inescapable shower of feathers and un-manna like offerings accompanying the spectacle.

Unfortunately no-one in the household had the heart to kill off the excess birds, not even Mother who suffered most of all from their activities. A badly needed cull would never have been achieved but for the irate complaint of Mr Steele from across the 'backs'.

Well versed of necessity to seize the moment with both hands, Mother arrested him in full tirade.

"You may wring the necks of any you can catch," she said, "and I'll be nothing but grateful to you."

He took her at her word and the good work commenced. Word spread around and before long he was not the only neighbour enjoying the occasional squab pie.

Numbers depleted, the pigeons became almost tolerable until, gradually, natural selection took a hand. The survivors became very hardy and very wary. So did their offspring. The neighbourhood catches became fewer and fewer and the depredations of the increasing Muck Birds greater and greater.

Finally they attacked the mortar between the bricks of the chimney, almost demolishing the stack. This was a strategic error on their part.

When Dad received the bill for repairs, Mother announced very bluntly that the Muck Birds had flown their last sortie.

She sold them all while the lads were at school and, on their return, handed Frank the money and Harry a shovel.

"Get up in that pigeon loft and clean it!" she said. "And don't leave as much as a feather to remind me of them!"

Shortly afterwards we moved house to a newly built semi-detached one in Atholl Avenue, where I began to take an interest in the smaller living creatures around.

Following the pigeon crisis, my modest interests seemed of very little significance and I could never understand the fuss that was made about the little peccadilloes of my pets. After all, what harm could possibly result from an interest in aquaria and their fishy inhabitants?

I could not afford to buy fish tanks so I made them from cement, reinforced with wire netting, and horticultural glass from Woolworths at three old pence a sheet. They were sufficiently ingenious in design to meet with approval and even encouragement from Mother, a rare accolade.

My first stock consisted of newts, diligently captured from the shallow ponds close to the goods sidings. They were magnificent. Great crested ones, yellow-bellied and spotted ones. I gloated over my collection, lovingly fed them tiny scraps of meat and furnished their tanks with water weeds and all the home comforts a newt could desire.

The honeymoon lasted a week. It ended with an angry yell from Mother. Arising at her customary early hour, she opened the scullery door upon a primeval scene in miniature spread over the quarry tiled floor.

My ungrateful newts had left their home during the night, crawled over the hollow worn step, under the door and into the house.

Torn unceremoniously from bed, I was somewhat brusquely told to gather up my filthy reptiles and return them forthwith to whence they came. Hungry and cold, I watched them swim away and walked back home to breakfast and a few pithy comments on my choice of pets.

However, the tanks did not remain empty for very long. Mother was very fair in all her dealings with us despite the tribulations we caused her. Indeed, her normal cynical strictness concealed a degree of pride and affection never revealed to anyone until we had all safely left home.

Anyway, what harm could a few fishes do? Swimming aimlessly around, unable to leave the water, they were nothing but decorative. No risk at all. Painstakingly I fished the local waterways for suitable varieties until my display was a matter of pride to all the family. Only Mother, wary from long experience, held any reservations in her approval.

All could have continued in this idyllic fashion but for the great-heartedness of Father who secretly sympathised with all our youthful enthusiasms. At that time he was driving the Coronation Scot, which involved an overnight stay in London; a 'double trip' in railway parlance.

With time to kill, each trip his knowledge of the capital became more remarkable, particularly of the lesser-known picturesque trivia of human interest. Among these latter was a Continental fresh fish shop selling imported live Dutch eels. There were tanks full of them, writhing and ready for purchase by the discerning customer who liked his fish truly fresh.

Father could not resist. He arrived home with four beautiful two footers, wriggling happily in a nest of wet moss and newspaper inside his meal basket. In an absolute transport of delight and gratitude, I installed my new specimens in the big zinc bath which housed my larger denizens.

They swam sinuously around, snapping up the worms I dug for them, the pride of my collection until one morning I found the bath empty. Desolated I searched fruitlessly for my slippery pets.

Father reassured me that they could not be far away and would turn up again where least expected. He was right. They did.

An almighty scream from Mother, normally so calm and self-controlled, announced the reappearance of one of them. The sight of it, writhing upwards from the bowl of the outside toilet at a crucial intimate moment, shattered even her remarkable equilibrium.

When she had finished demanding of the Almighty why she should be so afflicted, she talked to me somewhat loudly and critically. She did not neglect Father, either, in his role of eel supplier. My eels, the other three of which had turned up in the rainwater grid, were banished for good. After Mother's descriptions of them

I should think they were glad to go.

Somewhat chastened, I restricted my aquarist activities to less agile fish and all went well until my mates and I cycled to Hoylake for the day. Happily paddling around in the sea, studying the less mobile creatures, we found the crabs. Two green beauties, each the size of a clenched fist, with long grasping pincers and waving legs.

Temptation was too great. Into my saddle bag they went and back home with me. Wiser now, I told no-one. I mixed up the salt water in secret and installed a tank at the end of the garden.

After their disappearance the following morning, I lived in some anxiety for a couple of days and had just begun to breathe easily when I overheard Old Man Oliver conversing agitatedly with Mother.

"Just now," he announced breathlessly. "On my allotment! I was hoeing up the spuds when this 'orrible great thing scuttled across me foot and shot away along the row! A spider it must 'ave bin, but as long as this!" His shaking hands indicated something the size of a dinner plate. "Must have escaped from somewhere. I dursn't go back yet.'"

I walked nonchalantly past them into the house. Mother's eyes followed me speculatively.

"All right!" she said, when she came inside. "What was it this time?"

'Slings and Arrows...'

ather was a jovial, kind-hearted man and generous to a fault. But for Mother's restraining influence, his generosity and readiness to believe the best of everyone would have beggared us all. His hand dipped too readily into his pocket; he was a sucker for every hard luck story he heard.

Always ready to see the humorous side of things and possessing the rare ability to laugh at himself, his good nature stood him in good stead for he was surely one of nature's fall guys. If ever there occurred any sort of calamity entailing no drama or heroics but only the ludicrous, Father was sure to be near the centre of it. The most mundane of incidents or endeavours were apt to rebound upon him in the most undignified fashion, fortunately bouncing off his good-natured resilience like so many ping-pong balls. Full of humour, he was never humiliated by life's little perversities.

Even when halted at a main line signal, Father could not snatch a bite from a meat pie without hurling away his false teeth onto the embankment along with the offending gristle he had spat out.

The resulting spectacle of driver and fireman apparently searching diligently for nature's smaller wonders in the high grass must have diverted the passengers no end; especially when Father, with a shout of triumph, popped the teeth into his mouth and leaped to the footplate just in time to open the regulator as the signal changed.

Such minor incidents were frequent and trivial. Father also featured in several of life's grand spectacular productions designed to cut us sharply down to size. One such star performance depended upon a sequence of minor coincidences that only a very competent director of stage farce could deliberately contrive. Father seemed to attract such disastrous coincidences like a lodestone.

Awakening mid-morning, after returning late from a long 'double trip', he arose and began to descend the stairs. These were very steep and terminated in a large red-tiled entrance hall from which a wide front door opened onto a path and lawn.

By sheer chance, Mother, ten minutes or so previously, had started to carry downstairs the, then, ubiquitous chamber pot, with the intention of washing it. On the second step from the top she paused abruptly, remembering a promise made to see her neighbour about some matter of mutual interest.

Putting down the chamber pot on the tread where she stood, she walked downstairs and left by the front door, leaving it open for her return. Still sleepy, Father took the first step down towards the inevitable. Into the chamber pot went Father's foot, right past the rim and tightly wedged inside. Off the step it shot, and Father, flat on his back, complete with firmly attached jerry, thumped and slid his ignominious way downstairs.

The horrendous crash when he hit the hallway came from the exploding impact of the chamber pot upon the quarry-tiled floor. Father lay recumbent at the foot of the stairs, but the abundant fragments of broken jerry hurtled unimpeded along the hall, through the open doorway, to scatter across the front lawn before the startled gaze of the new neighbours in Atholl Avenue.

Fortunately, Father escaped injury and, as usual, philosophically looked for the bright side of things after his heroic glissade.

"At least it was empty," he said cheerfully.

Not long before we left Ruskin Road, Mother had rashly asked Father if there was anything he could do to renovate an ageing shelf supporting the various little-used mysteries that accumulate in most cellars.

We accompanied Father to the cellar to inspect the offending shelf. Even emptied of its burden the shelf sagged alarmingly and Father carefully removed it from the old wooden brackets on which it rested. The latter were thick sections of timber apparently set into the brickwork when the house had been built.

Since one of these was worm-eaten and loose it was decided that both should be removed and replaced with modern metal brackets.

Accordingly, I was dispatched to the ironmongers to obtain them whilst Father set about removing the wooden supports. On my return I was surprised to find him still struggling desperately with the first loose bracket.

"I can't understand it," he said. "The thing's so loose it ought to pull straight out."

He scraped more mortar from around the timber and vigorously wriggled it from side to side. Judging by the noises within the wall itself something had begun to dislodge but the support still would not pull clear.

"Stand back," warned Father, in as near an impatient voice as I ever heard from him, "I'm going to give it a good straight heave."

He braced his feet against the foot of the wall, seized the wooden bracket in both hands and threw his whole weight backwards in the pull.

With a protesting creak, the bracket gave a little. Father spat upon his hands and attacked it once more. This time it came out, not with a creak, but a thunderous crash from the opposite side of the wall. Somewhat nonplussed, Father stood looking at the timber in his hands. Not a short bracket, but a double one, shaped at both ends and stained by mortar in the centre where it had been built into the partition wall to support a shelf on both sides. It still held the twisted nails from the neighbour's side.

We were still regarding it in some dismay when we heard

someone running down the steps into the next door cellar. There was a moment of very pregnant silence; then, "Bloody hell!" announced a sepulchral voice from the other side of the wall.

Father applied his eye to the hole vacated by the bracket. Another eye regarded him balefully from the other side.

"What's going on then, Sam?" the voice continued. "The ruddy shelf's dropped off the wall and I'm knee deep in broken jam jars and spuds."

Father and his oppo continued their one-eyed appraisal for a moment or two and then both burst into laughter.

"Good job we're mates," the echoing voice managed to say at last. "Shove it back in and we'll cement it up from both sides before the missus comes back."

Mr Taylor came round after repairs had been effected.

"It's an ill wind," said Father. "We'll have a pint or two and a good laugh out of this at the club tonight!"

'Amor Vincit Omnia'

*F*rank being the first born of my brothers had all the advantages. Mother, rejoicing still in the blissful upbringing of a girl child, retained all her illusions. Within a year of Frank's appearance on the scene these had begun to tarnish and crack a little. By the time Harry and I entered the lists they had long disappeared and given way to an apprehensive and often cynical questioning of all our motives.

In a word, Frank, for a short while anyway, got away with murder. We seldom, if ever, escaped the consequences of those ploys which had eluded Mother's practised eye. More often, under her vigilance, our best plans were stillborn.

The effects of all this would have intrigued a psychologist. Certainly Frank's early successes, and his freedom from the wrath that inexorably overtook Harry and me, gave him a personal super confidence that we later additions to the family never possessed to anything like the same degree.

This confidence became increasingly apparent in his dealings with the fair sex. Much later, when I entered the mixed grammar school through which he had passed, the legend of 'Yanner' Morris and his amorous exploits still persisted. Time had swollen them to Casanova-like proportions and there were repercussions for me; but more of that later.

There were all the usual hot-eyed tales. Seduction in the boiler house, in the tower, even, word had it, at the back bench of a chemistry class. Ninety per cent pure embroidery, of course, but the main fabric remained and his greater romances were substantiated and still on record.

We were all very fortunate in having many quite idyllic areas for dalliance in the rural surroundings of our town. Such a place lay in the Mill Fields, a chain of green pastures circling the mill pond, linked by rustic stiles and bordered by conveniently concealing willows. It was here that Frank began and ended his first great affair.

Her name was Annie Adams and, to judge by her younger sister, a contemporary of mine, was somewhat substantial in build and stolid of character... Perhaps it was the contrast of the latter quality with his own mercurial temperament that attracted Frank. Whatever it was, he certainly made his conquest and the beginning of a legend. Expeditions to the Mill Fields became frequent and, according to hearsay, their flushed faces on return indicated more than mere zeal for their advanced biology course.

Confident and lucky Frank may have been, but the family tendency for all things to conclude in the spectacular and ludicrous dogged him too.

The lush meadows were well cropped by dairy cows and, in all but very dry weather, the areas around the field gates adjacent to the stiles were hoof-plodded into a glutinous morass of mud and worse. Small obstacles such as this had never daunted Frank. His confidence gave him a Raleigh-like courtesy that we all lacked, and gallantly enfolding the ample Annie into his arms as she balanced on the stile, he would carry her to the safety of dry grass with all the aplomb of an eighteenth century gallant.

Harry and I would have foreseen the inevitable outcome. Not Frank. He continued until the day when his foot slipped and gallantry deserted him. Instead of falling he regained his equilibrium by jettisoning his burden.

When Annie had finished scraping all she could of the clinging mud and cow-flop from her buxom charms, she rounded upon Frank, addressed him in a few well chosen if not ladylike phrases, and the romance was ended.

Maybe if Frank had not shared the family inability to conceal its emotions, things might have mended, but to roll about in apoplectic mirth whilst his beloved wallowed in the mud and dung... *Excreta Tauri Vincit Amor!*

Frank's next amatory exploit was unusual to say the least. On the outskirts of the town, surrounded by a high wall, stood a large foreboding brick building housing a sizeable community of nuns. There was a school attached and a fair number of novices or, doubtless, in Frank's eyes, a number of fair novices.

The latter were commonly to be seen taking the air, usually in pairs for mutual protection against the distractions of this wicked world. Sometimes they sat demurely on the wooden seats near to the convent walls.

It was only when one of the prettiest of the novices was observed sitting alone at one end of the seat with Frank at the other that the first breath of scandal was felt. Not that anything untoward was ever seen, but she was alone with but a few feet of bench separating her from the youth whose conversation raised unseemly blushes on her cheeks. In modern terms, Frank was chatting her up.

Rumour had it that these encounters were only the means of arranging more significant assignations and, in the case of my eldest brother, I cannot deny the possibility of this. Nevertheless, I am charitably inclined to believe that the affair was purely an academic exercise, a studied proof that no female was immune to his approaches.

If this was so, it can hardly have been worth the roasting he received from his headmaster when complaints from the convent appeared upon the latter's desk

On the other hand, the notoriety that followed; the reputation gained; the stimulated eagerness and curiosity of the sixth form girls! Perhaps it was.

Because of the improbable effect upon me at a much later date, one more of Frank's amorous interludes deserves a brief mention; or at least the abrupt conclusion thereof.

Obviously attracted by the lady's physical charms rather than her conversation, he suffered much. A would-be snob, she earbashed him unmercifully about the superiority of her home and family. He indulged her, presumably because of adequate returns, until she boastfully hinted at direct descent from Nell Gwynn.

This was altogether too much for Frank, tactless like all of us despite his amatory prowess.

"Well," said he. "If I'd been related to an infamous London whore, I'd keep it dark.'"

Remember! Remember!

November at the best of times is a dreary month, the very dog-end of the year with nothing to leaven its cold dankness. It was perhaps the depressing weather that caused Father's series of mishaps for, accident-prone as he normally was, four traumatic experiences in one week certainly exceeded his norm. No blame could be attached to him. Fate singled him out as though aware of his kindly tolerance and humour.

The month opened in a flurry of snow which overlaid everything to a depth ideal for snowballing and the various masochistic occupations beloved of the young. Amongst other bone chilling activities, we rolled an enormous snowball. It was almost a yard in diameter when we abandoned it because of the thick fog brought along by the approaching thaw.

Father, returning after midnight from a main line double trip, groped his way homewards from the loco sheds. The way was not yet familiar since we had only recently moved to the new house and, with some relief, he turned into our avenue; to promptly somersault over the abandoned snowball.

Picking up himself and meal basket with his usual philosophical acceptance of life's small rebuffs, he cautiously advanced through the murk.

Our semi-detached houses were very similar even by day. Chance could be blamed for directing his fog-bound footsteps to the wrong house. But not for choosing next door but one, and certainly not for the unlikely fit of Father's back door key into the lock.

Boots removed out of consideration for his sleeping family, he creaked his cautious way upstairs. Widow Weston's half-alarmed, half-hopeful query froze him on the top step. He tiptoed hastily down, cautiously relocked the door and fled for home in blind panic.

Mother's laughter as she comforted the trembling escapee awoke us all and it was a fair time before the last near hysterical chuckle ceased to shake the mattresses.

In the morning, mindful of the approaching Fifth, we made a guy. Jackets, overalls, boots and gloves, stuffed with straw, it was a splendid effort, lifelike and mobile of limb. Such artistry merited a better storage place than the open air.

Denied the house by Mother's indignant refusal we scouted round for suitable accommodation. Never lacking in imagination, we installed the guy upon the seat of the outdoor toilet which was seldom used.

Fate again made sport of Father. His night return, his consideration in not using the bathroom toilet to avoid disturbing the family, followed naturally. His shriek from outside as, in the dark, he dropped his nether garments and sat down upon the guy's lap, woke half the neighbourhood.

Good nature a little strained, Father drove us back to bed with harsh words. The springs rattled beneath our shaking forms. This time we dared not laugh aloud.

All forgiven by morning we left the house to fool around in the garden. As always, the game developed into football, strictly forbidden because of plants and windows.

Mother hastily despatched Father to restrain us. He spoke

sternly about the error of our ways. We stopped playing. The football lying between us proved irresistible. Father kicked it. Up it went, straight over the garden wall towards our neighbour's house.

The crash, as it passed through their dining room window and onto their breakfast table, brought out Mother at the double.

Her sympathy and loyalty to Father, already overstrained by the week's events, broke down.

"Get inside!" she said. "You're worse than the kids!"

Spiked!

n the early Thirties gunpowder could still be bought quite freely over the counter in any gunsmith's shop and even in some ironmongers where they sold cartridges as a sideline.

We lived in a farming county where, at least in the rural areas, shotguns were the normal mural decoration in most farmhouses and country cottages. Cartridges were cheap then but, even so, the more frugal sportsmen, reluctant to pay the price of tailor-made ones, refilled their own with black powder. Some of the guns, in any case, were too old to have been nitro-proved for modern propellants.

Black powder cost three old pence an ounce and was dispensed from a brass flask onto the scales and poured quite casually into whatever metal container the customer produced. No-one raised an eye-brow at the eleven or twelve-year-old lad buying powder for his father.

To the dismay of the neighbourhood we already made our own

fireworks, relatively harmless things which belched out stinking sulphurous clouds, but we had no access to real firearms. Even Uncle Harry drew the line at this and refused point blank to lend us his twelve bore.

I no longer recall who first thought of the loco boiler tubing so readily available in a railway town. Offcuts and discarded tubes lay in abundance around the loco building and repair shops. About an inch and a half in internal diameter, they were just the calibre for a small cannon and ready-made to withstand pressures.

An eighteen inch length of tubing was easily acquired. We thumped one end flat with a lump hammer, poured in a substantial two inch plug of molten lead and drilled out a touch hole. The cannon was made, black powder was available; we were in business.

The whole deadly apparatus was carried in secret to a derelict house outside the town. We poured a spoonful of powder down the barrel, rammed a thick wad of cloth on top, dropped in a large iron nut as a projectile, laid the cannon across a brick, business end directed towards a wall, and stood back.

The crucial question of ignition arose. For once we had no eager volunteers to apply a match. A pinch of powder on the touch hole, a strip of dry paper laid across it and all was ready for a proving shot. We tossed for the doubtful privilege of gunner and I lost.

Gingerly, I approached, applied flame to the extreme end of the paper strip and ran.

Safe round the corner we waited. The bang was impressive, so was the billow of blue smoke and the whirring sound of the cannon recoiling at speed.

Dashing round the corner, we eagerly inspected the wall. Half a brick knocked clean out of it! After a triumphant leap or two we searched for the cannon and eventually found it some fifty yards away, hot and smoking but undamaged.

Success raised our ambitions. We experimented with different projectiles and increased charges, becoming more and more casual as to the handling and discharge of our ordnance.

The last and biggest charge we fired in the centre of the largest field to which we could obtain access. It was well chosen for running but not so good for strategy since it backed onto the Police

Training College housed in the old Nunnery in the, then, outskirts of Crewe on the Nantwich Road.

Cannon triple loaded, primed and lit, we left it hurriedly and crouched down. The resultant explosion could literally be felt. There was a fair shock wave, birds shot up noisily from all around and the distant windows of the police building rattled in their frames.

Our delight was somewhat dashed when we entered the smoke cloud to find the scattered shards of our burst cannon everywhere; it was even more dampened by the sight of blue uniformed figures running across the field towards the pillar of smoke and us. We took to our heels, scattered and ran by devious ways back to our various homes.

Undaunted we constructed more cannon but used them discreetly and with greater respect. We made bombs too, out of lead water piping with both ends banged up on a central charge and touch hole. These were great fun until David Harpur lit the paper fuse just as a gust of wind blew it straight onto the priming.

Up went the bomb and the distressed David ran straight through the adjacent shallow pond, hands clasped to his eyes, shouting: "I'm blind! I'm blind!" Happily he was not but his face was permanently tattooed with blue specks from the black powder and our explosive pastime was terminated abruptly before we were all hoist with our own petard.

Cannon confiscated and pyrotechnics forbidden, our spectacular pastime came to an end but the firearm bug had bitten me hard. Secretly I collected the materials and constructed a .22 musket. In retrospect it seems quite an achievement for a twelve-year-old boy. I made the smooth bore barrel by cutting the required length from the right diameter tube and reinforcing it by wrapping it evenly in several layers of wire, each meticulously soldered solid. This hinged and locked onto a solid brass breech plate soldered into position and pierced for a rim fire pin. I adapted the pin release mechanism from the trigger and sear of an old air gun, the stock of which I also retained. Breech reamed out to take a .22 cartridge, and the thing was ready to fire.

Proving could not be done until all the family were out. I loaded and fired the first shot. It put a hole through a half inch plank and, thoroughly elated, I fired at every safe target in sight. Unfortunately these included apples on the tree next door.

There were no repercussions for several days and then Mrs Walker happened to mention to Mother that her apple crop had been attacked by some very queer grubs.

"They've eaten their way straight through," she said, "from one side to the other. I've never seen grub holes anything like these before."

"Queer!" responded Mother laconically.

"Very queer!" she reiterated when she came inside. "Where's that old air gun? Fetch it!"

When her eyes lit on the lethal weapon I had to produce she waxed lyrical for some time. After much demanding of heaven as to why any woman should be so plagued, she took my precious gun out to the coal house and spiked it for good with the coal hammer. In fact, she flattened every moving part of the mechanism and threw the bits in the bin.

Afterwards she proceeded to flatten me.

Plumbing the Depths

ortunately for us Mother never did discover why Mrs Walker became estranged and refused to speak to any of us for a month or more. Mrs Walker was our next door neighbour, a rather dignified elderly widow of impeccable if unassailed virtue. During this time, Harry and I, who were responsible for the rift, kept a very low profile.

On the whole our neighbours were very tolerant of the few activities that directly impinged upon their peace of mind. This was only reasonable since, gifted with a certain manual dexterity and ingenuity, we were quite often extremely useful to them in domestic emergencies. There were few households up and down the street that had not benefited at one time or another from a helping hand with minor electrical or mechanical problems, to say nothing of more mundane *coups de main*.

Mother looked upon these same talents with more apprehension than pride.

We were never lawless, violent or in any way disrespectful, but our practical ability in combination with unbounded imagination caused her constant speculation about our little ploys. She never worried very much on our account. "The devil looks after his own," she would affectionately say of us. It was the fringe effects that caused her a certain degree of unease.

She was absolutely right, of course; even when one of the many cannon we made recoiled across two back gardens and flew through Old Robinson's greenhouse. An immediate visit with glass, putty, hammer and nails put matters right within the hour and mollified him to the extent of searching his garden for the offending weapon. He did not find it and the following day brought home from work another length of L.M.S. boiler tubing for us to make another. Mother failed utterly to appreciate his forgiving nature and her remarks about this charitable act were anything but ladylike as she confiscated our new raw materials.

The practical services we rendered to our neighbours were with no exception completely successful and entailed none of the misfortune that seemed to dog every task undertaken at home. Halos well polished, we would set about some useful repair or modification to our own house, only to to have the whole situation recoil upon us like Old Robinson's cannon.

It was such a task, competently done with the best of motives that brought about the temporary alienation of Mrs Walker, a situation only relieved finally by her own need of our handiness.

Harry and I, whose large feet and innumerable footballs had been responsible for the flattening of the waste pipe from the kitchen sink, decided to replace it with a new length, thereby scotching any further recriminations when the sink refused to empty. We acquired the materials and awaited the opportunity to pleasantly surprise Mother with the accomplished repair.

With her safely out for the evening we set about the task, laboriously chipping out the pipe from the wall, unscrewing it from the sink and withdrawing it. This took longer than we expected and the evening was well advanced before we had sweated the new lead pipe onto the waste trap and were ready to offer up the assembled drain to the hole in the wall.

In the manner of many inanimate objects faced by a straightforward manipulation it refused to be pushed through the perfectly adequate hole vacated by the old pipe. We chipped out more of the wall by torchlight and tried again. Still it would not go and by this time daylight had completely gone.

"Try the blasted thing again," said Harry. "I'll run round with the torch to see what's stopping it."

He departed and I pushed valiantly at the pipe. Whatever was obstructing it suddenly broke away and the pipe shot through; the whole lot of it in one thrust. From the other side of the wall came a resounding crash and Harry's voice raised in blasphemy and anguish. His remarks on the subject of witless junior assistants who pushed out pipes into the paths of hurrying craftsmen were crude and pointed.

He was still groaning and lamenting loudly from the prone position when Mrs Walker threw up her bedroom window and leaned out, curlers gleaming in the moonlight. Roused from her early slumbers, she called reproachfully, "Harry. I'm in bed!"

Pain dispelled discretion. "Right you are, Mrs Walker," he retorted, "I'll be up in a minute!"

There was a moment of horrified silence before the window slammed down.

Mother speculated for long enough as to how she had offended Mrs Walker. Neither of us dared to enlighten her.

Uncle Harry

ncle Harry's rambling old house held an irresistible fascination for me. It was stuffed with Victorian *bric à brac* and curious objects brought back from his extensive wanderings. There was always the faintly musty smell of old furniture, wax polish, pipe tobacco and, over-riding all of these, a faint heady smell of beer and spirits. The old scoundrel, who was then on the edge of his eighties, loved to be surrounded by reminders of his colourful youth.

Because of Uncle Harry's forthright speech and his supposed bad influence upon us, we were severely discouraged from visiting him too often, but I went in spite of this. There was always a welcome, a good tale or two and even a drop of ale on the sly.

My Aunt Lizzie came originally from Abergavenny and her high Welsh voice had a piercing quality that screeched like an unoiled hinge. It screeched incessantly except in the presence of Uncle Harry. Then it lowered several octaves and fell dramatically in volume and tempo.

It was perhaps this voice which had prompted Uncle Harry, in the 1880s, to quit his engineering post in the loco works, leave his young bride in England and sail away to a job in Venezuela where he pioneered in the building of the first railway in that country, from Caracas to Quebrada.

I still have in my possession a metal daguerreotype of a young bewhiskered Uncle Harry seated on a cane chair, apparently in thick jungle if one is to believe the background, one hand holding a rifle, the other on the handle of a sheathed machete dangling from his belt, and his eyes fixed firmly on infinity.

Although the allowance to his young bride had always been more than adequate, the family had strongly disapproved of his sudden unseemly departure for the New World. Even his eventual return with a more than modest fortune, strange outlandish habits and a bright green parrot, failed to mollify his relations, though Aunt Lizzie herself is reported to have welcomed him back with open arms and, I imagine, an appropriately loud screech.

My forbidden visits were a great delight to me. He and the, now ancient, parrot belonged to a bygone age. The parrot was capable of out-screeching Aunt Lizzie but it never dared. Its training was very thorough. One squawk out of place and a miniature cane was hung upon the perch. Two squawks merited application. The aggrieved parrot would swear heartily in Spanish and Uncle Harry replied in kind. Cane in hand, he always had the last word.

It spoke little English and that only on the occasion of the local curate's weekly visits to Aunt Lizzie. Coached by its anti-cleric master it always bade the reverend gentleman welcome in very basic four letter Anglo-Saxon.

Having suitably embarrassed both Auntie Lizzie and the curate, Uncle Harry would produce the cane, hang it on the perch and depart, laughing heartily, to leave them to their religious discussions.

The curate must have been a man of great devotion and spirit to have continued his weekly visits for, apart from ordeal by the parrot, he still had to undergo the trial of Aunt Lizzie's formidable wines.

She made them by the barrel from all manner of wholesome fermentable materials. They were wines not to be confused with the tamed, emasculated drinks sipped and savoured today in suburban wine-making circles. Uncle Harry started off each brew with a bottle of whisky poured into the small cask. Then Aunt Lizzie took over. The very palatable, but fiery, end product snatched away the breath of the incautious consumer.

Aunt Lizzie herself never touched the stuff and, consequently, had no idea of seemly quantities to pour. Duly welcomed by the parrot, the curate had thrust before him an immense slab of saffron cake and a large tumblerful of her firewater. Frequently the poor man would lurch tipsily past the crates of ale standing in the hallway and head back to the vicarage with all other visits abandoned.

Always ready to sample new experiences, Uncle Harry had a multitude of electrical gadgets to alleviate his rheumatic twinges. They ran from a bank of enormous dry batteries: shockers, vibrators, wigglers and muscle contractors. He used them all without the slightest faith or beneficial result. I played for hours with them, turning up the power till the universe vibrated round me.

He also possessed a newfangled wireless set, a marvellous black box surmounted by six glowing red-capped valves and with three huge graduated dials on the front. The tinny sounds it produced emerged from a tall curved horn loudspeaker. Uncle Harry was by no means an avid listener though the apparatus was usually left switched on. There were not many broadcasts with which he agreed and whenever the speech or music aroused his displeasure he would retort somewhat crudely and silence the offending sound by thrusting a large red handkerchief violently down the throat of the horn speaker. Evidently this gave him much greater satisfaction than flicking a switch. I hesitate to imagine what he would have done in this age of television and even more moronic programmes. I fancy the local dealer would have made a fortune in replacement tubes, since there was always a double-barrelled twelve bore decorating Uncle Harry's wall.

Neighbours eyed him askance because of this same shotgun. Even in old age, some Venezuelan influence lingered on and his disconcerting habit of flinging up the window to discharge both barrels at trespassing animals did not endear him to them. Redress was often difficult. Uncle Harry shot and fished with the Chief Constable.

He always gave me the radical advice that mother feared. "Don't listen to 'em." he would say. "Cram in everything you can, boy. You've not long to fit it all in. It's not what you've done you'll regret, but all the things you've not done! By God! I've done them all!" and he would chortle with recollected pleasure. "Remember, lad, the only sure thing in life is death. Make sure it doesn't beat you!"

When Aunt Lizzie died, Uncle Harry was a broken man; but not for long. His affection had been sincere and deep but he was not a man to ignore his own advice.

Before long he thrust his sorrow behind him and resumed his old way of life. The family, already disapproving of so short a mourning period, repudiated him entirely when barely two months elapsed before the installation in his house, and bed, of a personable young lady a third of his age.

"What else do they expect me to do?" he said to me. "I'll be damned if I'm going to start cooking at my age, and I get cold feet at night."

The family withdrew in shock. His face was turned to the wall. No more despicable creature ever sullied the family name. The whole subject was forbidden. As for the Scarlet Woman, the Hussy who lived with him! Lips were pursed at the thought of such immorality.

My visits now were made only by extreme stealth and sub-terfuge. I found his lady love very pleasant and even sweet voiced after poor Aunt Lizzie's screech. Besides, she fed me well on all the unwholesome confections I liked. Loaded with advice from Uncle Harry and sweets from his paramour, I used to creep guilti-ly home after each clandestine visit.

Unhappily, this state of affairs continued for little more than a year. Inevitably, the sudden resumption of all his youthful activi-ties proved too much even for Uncle Harry. He expired suddenly, in embarrassing circumstances it was rumoured. If there was any truth in this he died very happily, just as he would have wished.

Gloomily, the family prepared themselves for the ultimate

insult, the reading of his will. The thought of house and property in the hands of that hussy soured the most charitable of them. They brooded round the grave like thwarted vultures as the black sheep was laid to rest.

Dead Uncle Harry's smile must have widened vastly at the reading of the will. Within five minutes not a female eye was dry. How cruelly they had misjudged him! His virtues, his manliness, his fortitude were extolled. Not a halfpenny had he left to his lady love. All was willed to the family, his own kith and kin. A truer man never lived!

It was much too late to recant when the estate resolved into unfinished mortgages and unpaid debts. Lady love had collected in advance. Uncle Harry had always favoured cash on delivery himself. The cupboard was bare.

My cousin Peg came out best. She had the parrot. I envied her greatly. It might have survived long enough to keep me reminded of Uncle Harry's sound advice.

Desperate Remedy

*F*rank's luck was phenomenal. Where Harry and I fell metaphorically base over apex into the mire and picked ourselves up smelling of the same, Frank would arise smelling sweetly of nothing worse than aftershave lotion. Even his literal falls carried the same good fortune, as when he slid down the roof of his house, which he was repairing at the time, shot out into space and descended some forty feet in a rapid parabola into his newly dug rose bed.

His wife heard the thud but, well experienced in her husband's little eccentricities, waited for him to walk round to the door to explain the latest mishap. He limped very slightly and bore one or two rose thorn scratches, it is true, but these were nothing to justify his bitter complaints about the tiles broken during the dramatic descent.

My sister-in-law was very long-suffering. Warned by my mother of the hazards and tribulations likely to follow upon marriage into our family, she felt bound, I suppose, to make the best of it. Fortunately, Ethel had already had some little experience of her own brother's accident-prone nature. He, poor chap, seemed destined to receive the dirty end of life's stick but with unfailing good nature managed always to reverse it.

Around the time of Frank's fall from the roof, Ethel's brother had risen very shakily from his sick bed and made his first unaided visit to the toilet since his illness. Still shivering with weakness, he pulled on the chain from the seated position. With the impeccable timing reserved for the butts of life's small jokes, the brackets retaining the cistern pulled out of the wall. The cistern fell away in a slow descent, still attached to its lead pipes, struck him on the head with sufficient force to stun him and continued to drench his seated form until he was rescued some fifteen minutes later.

Despite this, Ethel's brother still maintained his recovery rate and much later was accepted as air crew into the wartime Royal Air Force. His family accepted his disappearance into the Pacific Ocean with great fortitude. Even when he was later reported as presumed dead they dismissed such uninformed speculation as frivolous. "He'll turn up like a bad penny," they said.

They were absolutely right. He did after the end of the Far Eastern War. His whole air crew had spent the remaining war years, after their forced landing on the beach of a tiny island, enjoying the hospitality of the native inhabitants.

As a consequence of these factors Ethel had great forbearance. Only once did I see her lose patience and then, poor woman, she had two of us to contend with.

On that occasion I was still in the unlovely, gangling, trip-over-feet stage of early adolescence and had journeyed over to Manchester to spend a week with Frank and Ethel, a kindness on their part to give my own family a little relief.

Ethel's tolerance and smile did not even fade at the odd broken dish or two a day consequent upon my arrival in the household. She was a prudent woman and her standard practice was to store safely away all valuable breakables when younger in-laws were due to arrive.

It was plain misfortune that she should fall ill and retire to bed on the second day of my visit. Frank and I were very considerate in the matter of noise and we prepared breakfast without any clattering of dishes at all. True, the smell of burning toast and the spluttering fumes from the frying pan, when it caught fire, caused the invalid to querulously inquire whether she should vacate her bed before or after the fire brigade arrived, but this we put down to the unreasonable anxieties which beset the sick.

Nothing was said about the overflowing sink as we reassured her that the flames were all quenched, everything was completely under control and we were about to commence the daily housework. This latter intention seemed to strangely agitate Ethel and she pleaded with us to confine any further activities to repairs and maintenance on the car. To humour her we retired to the garage and began work on the gearbox which had been touchy for some time.

It was bitterly cold as we dropped out the transmission prior to the removal of the gearbox and, once it was detached and portable, by mutual agreement we hefted it into the warmth of the house.

Since the kitchen table was of the folding type and liable to collapse under an abnormally heavy weight, we laid the gearbox on the lounge carpet in front of the fire, prudently placing a newspaper or two beneath it. In comfort and warmth we stripped down the box before breaking off for lunch.

Strenuous work had given us healthy appetites and we laid the kitchen table well. It was no slovenly one plate and mug effort. We set all the necessary dishes and cutlery for gracious living. There was plenty of space for this. The table hinged from the wall supported, when in use, by one stout folding leg. When erected there was a considerable surface area, and we used all of it. Ethel, we felt, would have been proud of us.

She was surprised and delighted with the well-filled tray I took in to her. It was a great pity that she should call for the salt just as we sat down to eat.

Anxious to please even more, I leaped to my feet, knocking the folding leg aside in my haste. The resultant crash, deluge of smashing crockery and the anguished howls from Frank as the hot stew penetrated his flies, brought Ethel down from her bedroom at extraordinary speed for an invalid.

"I'm better!" she shouted, grabbing a broom. "I'm cured! Get out of my way!" Her new-found energy increased tenfold when she saw the dismantled gearbox and the oil that had seeped through the newspaper into the cream carpet.

"Out!" she cried. "Out! Take it out! I'll never be ill again!"

It did not seem to console her any when I ventured to suggest that we had apparently worked a miracle cure. The things she said about our family were most unreasonable. After all, she now carried the name herself.

Wilberforce

A boy's eternity had passed since the Muck Birds and the more bizarre pets had run their course in our scheme of things. At least two years had elapsed and we had moved in the meantime to a semi-detached house on the very edge of town.

My only remaining pet was an ancient and very friendly white rabbit who had survived all the vicissitudes that had beset us both since I was six years old. Now in extreme old age, he was still bright of eye and hearty of appetite, though limping somewhat because of rheumatism.

As befitted an old retainer, his hutch was well modified to suit his maturity. There were shutters to close out the cold night air, a double floor to ensure he was always dry, mountains of straw and, most important of all, a man sized stone hot-water bottle wrapped in flannel that was inserted under the straw each cold night.

The welcome he gave to this hot-water bottle was ecstatic. He would leap arthritically about the hutch whilst it was being installed and, if he thought I was a little late bringing it, the old chap would seize the bars of the hutch door between his teeth and rattle away until I appeared.

When the warm summer days favoured his old bones, he would walk around the garden, following anyone of the family like a small pet dog. The degree of affection in which he was held could be measured by Father's restraint whenever he nibbled the shoots of the prize carnations, a delicacy to which he was particularly partial.

Thus, when he finally fell ill, the whole household was concerned. He developed a cough which, in spite of the teaspoons of sugared brandy and the snug flannel coat with which Mother supplied him, grew steadily worse.

When I took him to the vet, wrapped in a green blanket, my feet were leaden. I think I already felt that the journey was one way.

The vet listened to his laboured breathing, lifted him and looked at him silently for a moment or two.

"You're an ancient old fellow," he said softly, one finger scratching tenderly between the drooping white ears. He turned to me.

"I can't do anything for the poor old beast, lad. He's over a hundred in human life span. Let me put him down, will you?"

I nodded, too full to speak, and whilst the vet gently applied the chloroform I stroked the white fur till the last tremor ceased.

The good man refused my proffered shilling, patted my shoulder, tucked the blanket under my arm and pushed me quietly out of the surgery. I didn't cry till I reached home, and nobody saw me.

Old Bunny, he never had any other name, left a vacuum and I imagine it was this that prompted the purchase of Wilberforce.

I'd cycled over to a nearby market town where, every Thursday, all things rural were on display for sale. One could buy anything from a chain harrow to wellington boots or a clutch of eggs. Poultry was sold all along the pavement at the entrance to the market hall and it was there that I saw Wilberforce, A double handful of yellow fluff, peeping heartily as he trampled over his fellow ducklings.

I bought the two-week-old extrovert for sixpence, stuffed him down the neck of my shirt and set off homewards. Apart from leaving his sticky trademark on my vest, he behaved well on the journey, surveying the world from the region of my collar bone and commenting now and again with an interested peep.

The family viewed my purchase with a deal of derision, airing the customary doubts as to my suitability to be at large in a sane society. Both my brothers progressed to conjecture on the subject of growth rate and argued heatedly about the respective merits of apple stuffing and sage and onion. Mother pointed out, in no uncertain terms, the incompatibility of a suburban back garden and a duckling. Having said her piece, she spent the best part of the day helping me to install Wilberforce in comfortable quarters.

"Thank God," she said fervently, "They don't fly!"

I think the memory of the Muck Birds was still evergreen.

Wilberforce made himself at home. Within an hour he had trampled his little pen into a morass of mud in which he squelched happily up and down, peeping merrily. His first bowl of crushed corn disappeared almost as fast as we could pour it in and we soon discovered that this was his normal rate of consumption.

Apart from an intense dislike of water – he complained hysterically when put into a bath of it – his progress was normal if rapid. His yellow down gradually became scruffily interspersed with white feathers which seemed to stick out at every conceivable angle. He had reached the hobbledehoy stage, an unlovely period in any ambulant creature. His voice broke too, changing from a gentle endearing peep-peep to a raucous strangled croak.

Quite undismayed by his inability to achieve an adult quack, he practised assiduously, giving tongue unceasingly as he followed Father's spade, hurling back worms as fast as they could be thrown to him.

It was these penetrating vocal efforts that brought about his first departure from our midst. Mother returned from a shopping and gossiping foray with an expression boding good to no-one.

"He's got to go!" she announced with no preamble. The family waited, each son searching his conscience for a reason to be shown the door.

"In the Co-op," she expanded, "they're all grumbling about the weird noise that wakes them up in the early morning. Some sort of bird they reckon it is. I said I'd heard it too. Sounded like a corn crake. And that's no lie. Get him away to Barnett's farm. Now!"

Wilberforce was unceremoniously thrust into a basket, slung on my handlebars, and away we went. Disconcerted by the unfamiliar motion he crouched in the bottom of the basket in most uncharacteristic silence. Halted at the Mill Street junction by the policeman on point duty, Wilberforce, equilibrium restored, chose to exercise his new voice.

After the constable had finished informing me at length of the penalties to be incurred by ignorant young louts who made derisory noises at officers of the law performing their duties, I hastily pedalled to the farm at Coppenhall, long since disappeared beneath a housing estate.

"Now there's a problem," said Doug slowly. "We've no ducks at the moment." There was a long pause. Doug never hurried important decisions.

"We can try him in with the hens if you like. He looks cocky enough."

Protesting loudly, in a flurry of moulting down, Wilberforce was introduced to his exile home. The ensuing hullabaloo rocked the hen house. Feathers drifted from the ventilators and a bedraggled Wilberforce shot out and headed at incredible speed for the farmhouse, croaking wildly in incredulous shock.

"Too young yet," pronounced Doug. "Give him a few weeks more."

The ruffled problem child squatted silently in his basket on the return journey, no doubt brooding over his experiences, but I took no chances with irate policemen and made a suitable detour.

The prodigal's return was not greeted with joy.

"I'll give him a fortnight," Mother threatened. "Then he goes back to the farm or into the oven."

Life took on a furtive aspect. It was rather like trying to conceal a very extrovert and mentally afflicted relation from the neighbours. Ingenious cover stories, offering possible explanations of the extraordinary noises, were leaked out to the folks around.

Two days before the ultimatum expired, Mother spotted two of her acquaintances standing near the front gate, heads cocked to one side, listening to Wilberforce's unmelodious efforts. She hastened out to them.

"You've heard it too?" she queried. "It can't be far away. Sounds as though it's in one of the back gardens!"

A little discussion about the possible identity of the ornithological freak and she came indoors.

"That's it! He goes. This instant!"

With no possibility of appeal, Wilberforce, now decked wholly in white feathers, was ignominiously bundled off back to the farm.

With a deal of trepidation, Doug and I pushed him into the hen house. Dismayed to hear even greater sounds of strife than before, we stood by to rescue the fugitive when he emerged.

The trap crashed open. Out flew the hens, fighting and jostling to escape, and out shot Wilberforce in hot pursuit. He paused, emitted a true quack, and waddled back to his new home.

"He'll do," said Doug. "Leave him there."

A mate was found for Wilberforce. A handsome Aylesbury duck rejoicing in the name of Pansy.

In the circumstances it was rather a let down for all concerned when Wilberforce laid her first egg.

Fallen from Grace

*F*ollowing in the path of my elder brothers through grammar school proved, as at home, to be a great disadvantage to me. The wake of their passage still rocked my boat from time to time even after the lapse of some eleven years.

I found that teaching staff, glancing casually in my direction, were apt to take a second sharper look and remark resignedly or threateningly, according to their styles:

"What? Another of your family? I thought we'd seen the last of them!" or, "Let's all hope you prove to be like your sister!"

Early training in the hard school of Mother's verbal appraisals had well proofed my broad back and such honeyed words of welcome ran off like water from a duck. It was with my peers that the impossibility of measuring up to legends, grown over the years to epic proportions, multiplied life's small stumbling blocks.

This particularly applied to any relationship with girls whose sisters had been contemporaries of Frank. Fed on apocryphal tales of 'Yanner' and his alleged exploits, their expectations terrified me; especially as, at this time, my only dalliance with the opposite sex had been a brief hand-clasping romance with a pretty black haired nine-year-old appropriately named Myrtle Raven.

Former junior beauty queen of the local Park Fete, she had brought me considerable prestige even amongst our primary school gang of hardbitten misogynists. The affair withered before the far greater attractions of fishing, hurling duck-stones, raiding and other gentle pastimes which preoccupied my social circle.

Around a gangling thirteen, puberty and proximity inducing the normal glandular responses, female characteristics ceased to be academic physical facts and became objects of absorbing interest. Since these fascinating zones were definitely 'no-go' areas without the time consuming ritual of admiration and declarations of undying affection, our innumerable calf loves began.

This phase persisted for a few years and each affair was usually short-lived and invariably non-productive. I recall but one clearly, a tepid liaison with the rather moon-faced Jenny Adams who dramatically terminated the innocent idyll on realising, belatedly, my relationship with 'Yanner the monster' who, having thrown her elder sister literally into the mire, stood by convulsed with mirth. Younger sons have always sucked upon the hind tit but never more so than in our family.

It was three years before I fell hopelessly in love with Grace. She was tall, broad-hipped and talked 'posh'. By some quirk of memory I cannot recall the precise colour of her hair, though other features I remember with extreme clarity.

Beyond doubt this was true love, for she was a gifted soprano and my adoration continued throughout all the many occasions when her top notes pierced my lamentably unmusical ears like the screech of metal on a window pane.

Never before had I so devoted my time and energy to the pursuit of a girl. She lived several miles away, and I would walk her home and face the return journey, with aching feet and memories of the outward bound embraces vying with each other for supremacy.

Eventually I was introduced to her mother who, although an excellent lady and devoted parent, frightened the living daylights out of me by the cold unemotional manner of her address. That and the uncanny resemblance to Grace. Perhaps a deep subconscious thought, 'Like mother, like daughter' ?

Anyhow, the only time I again attempted to call upon the lady a great Dalmatian dog, barking ferociously, hurtled from the driveway into the front wheel of my bicycle. Picking myself up from the gravel, on which I had made a five point landing, hands, knees and face, after a brief but dramatic somersault over the handlebars, I decided that blood, grime and torn trousers, though accepted philosophically at home, were not *comme il faut chez* Grace. Straightening out my handlebars, I pedalled thoughtfully home, a little relieved maybe at having suffered the lesser of two ordeals and with a lasting dislike of Dalmatians.

Grace sang in the choir of one of the lesser-known non-conformist sects, and on many occasions I paid for my post-service dalliance with devout attendance. This was often profitable but, in the end, it was religious zeal, or rather a lack of it, that seriously threatened my love life.

A Dr Woodford, or some such name, a national pillar of the particular sect, interrupted his circuit to conduct a midweek revivalist meeting in the chapel. Attendance obviously was a 'must', and since the choir was not operative Grace sat beside me.

Also present and sitting directly behind me was the son of the local preacher, an unprincipled lad rejoicing in the name of Andrew Baker-Long. Pious in appearance and upbringing, his dual personality was a byword in school. No doubt by now he is firmly and comfortably entrenched in politics or the teaching profession.

The service began well. With a suitably pious face I attended to the reverend gentleman's interminable address and sang lustily through 'The Old Rugged Cross' and other hymns, particularly those to which I knew other less fervent verses. As the climax approached we swung into a deafening rendering of "At the Cross, at the Cross, where I first saw the Light...", and at this juncture Andrew poked me in the back and sang, poker-faced, into my ear:

"Won't be long now, mate. You're in for it tonight."

He knew all right. When the echoes of the rousing hymn had

died away, amid the muffled sobs of the repentant, a resonant voice from the pulpit urged all those who were 'saved' to stand up as a testimony to everyone. Several stood, including Grace and the versatile Andrew. Again we were exhorted to stand and many more joined the upright and virtuous. Once more the plea boomed out and only I and one harassed-looking little man remained impiously seated. I felt and, no doubt looked, rather like one of Bateman's little men.

Andrew again poked me in the back and, with the salvation look still on his face, whispered urgently in my ear: "Stand up you silly bastard, and you'll be all right on the way home! Stay there and you won't get as much as a sniff."

This delicate message conveyed, his lips moved again in silent prayer.

He was dead right of course. I did get nothing on the way home except an earful about my lack of zeal and salvation. Evidently the heat of our mutual affection had fallen several degrees during my sit-in at the conclusion of the meeting.

A few lessons from Andrew and a little more tact on my part might yet have saved the day if, on the following evening, a mixed party of us had not attended a local show. Grace was not present and I could find no harm in embracing a curvaceous young lady whose ideas obviously did not include my salvation.

Matters were clinched by David Hayes, a musical type, who, having designs himself on the fair Grace, shopped me well and truly the following day.

I owe him much. The curvaceous lady in question and I enjoyed many hours of uncomplicated pleasure together and, years later, to the great astonishment of all our friends and the unbounded delight of my Mother, she relieved the latter of her last burden by marrying me.

The Not So Innocents Abroad

*T*he 'Chonks' were twins, the only remnant of the old gang to accompany me to college. Known respectively as 'Little Chonk' and 'Big Chonk', they too were the young afterthought of a family of brothers and, as such, talked and thought on much the same wavelength as myself.

I was still apt to decide on a course of action with little thought about means or ability, and so it was when I decided to cycle to the Mediterranean during the summer vacation. Now in those remote days this was travel indeed and everyone concluded that I was mad, with perhaps the exception of my mother, in whose memory my infantile trips to the Iron Bridge and other remote spots still lingered.

At the last moment the 'Chonks' became interested in my project and tentatively asked if they could join the venture. I welcomed their company provided that my planned route was to be in no way modified. Since they wished to see several places that did not figure on my itinerary we agreed to separate from time to time and to rejoin at prearranged places and dates. The fact that they had no passports was easily solved by their eldest brother, Professor Challenor of Manchester University, who was in a position to have their application forms signed and to present them in person for a rapid processing.

There were, of course, a few small snags. We had no money and only two bikes between the three of us. The second problem we solved first by a visit to the corporation rubbish tip. Here a frugal corporation, still bearing the scars of the Thirties depression, sorted their disposable refuse into piles, the scrap-iron heap being always at the disposal of equally frugal citizens prepared to pay a nominal sum for their choice of metal oddments.

The Chonks and I spent an afternoon sorting through the incredible variety of ferrous rubbish, emerging at last with a reasonably straight frame, handlebars, forks, pedals, wheels and indeed all the other separate components required except the mudguards. Complete with a mouldy leather saddle and part-worn tyres from another heap, we bore our rusty treasures to the office.

Officialdom required so long to list the scrap in triplicate that we became increasingly uneasy about the possible final costing. At last the clerk raised his head.

"Five pence the lot," he said.

We fished around in our pockets, paid up and departed in triumph. A whip-round of all our current wealth sufficed to purchase mudguards and pay for a little necessary welding to be done on the frame. Scraped, cleaned, painted, assembled and oiled the bike stood ready, even rejoicing in a name that had emerged from beneath the grime on the frame. It was a 'Hopper.' An accounting of total cost resulted in the staggering sum of three shillings and two pence.

Finances for the trip were more difficult and required delicate negotiations. Prolonged arguments with our families finally produced some of the normal cost of our keep during the holidays. After dispensing some of this on passports and customs triptyches for the cycles we were left with three pounds ten shillings per head to last for six weeks. The ten shillings just covered our 'quarter fare' passage from Dover to Calais on a railway boat.

We set off on the day we left Crewe Grammar School for the summer vacation, heavily laden with everything edible and durable that we could scrounge.

All went very well. We traversed Paris unscathed by the many exotic dangers against which we had solemnly been warned. Chance would have been a fine thing on our budget! Most disappointing.

On leaving Paris the Chonks and I diverged. They wished to see Chartres and Limoges; I had planned to ride over the Massif Central via Orléans, Bourges and Clermont-Ferrand. A few days later we met as planned at Montelimar, rode together as far as Avignon, and separated again since I wanted to visit Marseille before following the coast road along the Cote d'Azur to Monaco whilst they rode via Aix direct to Cannes. We met again at Monaco.

It was on the first leg of this ride that I foolishly ate a number of huge and delicious elderberries that were as ripe and sweet as any grapes. An hour or later I curiously observed that the landscape was swaying slightly but with increasing tempo and the sky had developed a peculiar futuristic zig-zag pattern. Incapable of riding by the time I reached the next village, I sat miserably upon the edge of the war memorial retching violently to the great interest of the local children. They did however give me the invaluable advice to seek help at the nearest farm where an incredibly kind farmer's wife took pity on the scruffy-looking, very sick, foreigner.

Bedded down in the clean thick straw of a closed barn, moaning and clutching my gut, I did not see the approach of the lady until she released the belt of my shorts and forcibly yanked them down to my ankles. My pants went with them and, modestly clasping both hands to my privates like a startled virgin, I stared wildly about in some confusion.

"There's nothing there I've not seen before in many sizes, my little one," she announced with a bosom-shaking laugh, and, tearing away my modest grip with one hand, she slapped a hot flannel-wrapped brick on my abdomen. Helpless with confusion and burning belly, I gave in while she pulled up my nether garments, tucked in my shirt, dropped a blanket on me, patted my cheek and departed with a *"Ça ira mieux, mon chou!"*

She was right. I was weak but ambulant by daybreak and able to take coffee and bread with her family at breakfast. Not a sou would she take for her kindness but tucked a loaf, a cheese and a bottle of red wine in my saddle bag instead and sent me on my way.

At Montelimar the Chonks and I exchanged tales of our experiences and continued as far as Avignon before separating. Still riding southwards, sleeping anywhere that was warm and sufficiently sheltered, I reached Marseille and found myself in the dock area at dusk. Not the most salubrious of districts and certainly an unlikely place to find a Youth Hostel, a luxury normally beyond our means. I was very relieved to see the familiar 'Auberge de Jeunesse' sign over a dockside building.

Pushing my bike thankfully inside, I received a distinctly boisterous welcome from a group of swarthy and seemingly unusually mature youth hostellers, redolent of garlic and red wine. I proffered my membership card. It was duly inspected, passed from hand to hand, admired and handed back to me with many complimentary remarks in an almost incomprehensible French on the excellence of the photograph on it. A heavy arm was flung round my shoulders and I was ushered inside where the strangest collection of young tourists gave a raucous shout of welcome.

Not one was younger than thirty; all were speaking in Spanish.

Even my slow thought processes began to register that something was not all it should be. In very slow French I asked if this really was the Youth Hostel.

No professional comedian could have produced a more satisfactory howl of mirth.

It had indeed been such a place, I was told, now it was temporary accommodation for refugees from Franco's Civil War.

Thanking everyone with careful politeness, I turned to go. Instantly my way was firmly barred. "Here we go again", I thought, "You've got yourself into the mire once too often this time." A hand relieved me of my pack, a grinning Spaniard was literally kicked off his bunk, his belongings thrown after him and, with an almost courtly grace, the villainous looking character holding my pack laid it on the bunk and offered me accommodation for the night. Urged by the dispossessed but still very amiable type, I sat on the bed. A plate of heavily garlicked beans and a glass were thrust into my hands. Whilst I ate a voluble group quizzed me about all things English.

The red wine flowed all evening and the following morning I parted from my hospitable friends wobbling slightly in the saddle but still very happy.

We met as planned at Monaco and turned our backs to the Mediterranean to head for the Rhône Valley and the route northwards together.

We'd not gone far before real disaster struck. Big Chonk's bike collapsed, quite irreparably, with the frame snapped in two places. Just a crack, a thump, and there he sat in the roadway with the forepart on one side of him, linked only to the rear section by the brake cable across his thighs. Ironically it was not the five-penny Hopper that broke but the other bike.

Heaving the debris into the ditch and shouldering his bags, Big Chonk prepared to hitch hike to pre-arranged destinations where we would meet him. During the following days we grew a little weary of arriving dog-tired to find that a fresh unexercised Big Chonk had already been chatting up the local talent for a couple of hours or so.

We were sixty miles from the Channel when the ultimatum was issued to Germany and, war inevitable, we broke all records to Calais, helped somewhat by hanging onto the backs of French army trucks moving in convoy to the coastal gap in the Maginot Line.

Two days' wait and we were over and home. Very unjustly Mother swore that the entire outbreak of war was undoubtedly due to the blighting effect of our presence in Europe. Like the prophet, we were never appreciated in our own country.

Gaudeamus and All That

That Frank should still remotely affect my progress through college was entirely my own fault. I could have chosen another one to grace with my presence. Fortunately, unlike school, the students were drawn from all regions of the country and, with two exceptions, had refreshingly never heard of 'Yanner.'

Not so the kitchen staff and waitresses in hall, one of whom, considerably my senior, gave me a long hard look on the first day, politely asked my name, and stridently warned the junior waitresses,

"Watch this one! I knew his brother!" Switching to me, she whispered, "I knew him all right. Tell him Bette sends her love."

Apart from this, I could not seriously complain though I was mildly shocked to discover that one of my younger tutors had also been a girlfriend of Frank during their school days together. She gave me a quizzical look or two but that was all. I thought her very generous not to visit the sins of the elder brother upon his cadet.

Life at college was good and passed very quickly with one or two high spots worthy of mention. Never a quarrelsome type myself, I do not think I ever knew quite how I came to fight with Donald. No doubt it was some breach of tact on my part. I was never noted for it.

He was a tall lean chap, a physical training fanatic, given to leaping energetically around the gym and running for miles round the district to go nowhere. Just to watch him made me feel tired. He shadow boxed with the most beautiful footwork one could ever see. His skill at boxing was considerable and his room contained juvenile cups to prove it.

As I said, I have no idea why, but Donald challenged me to a grudge fight, rounds unnumbered.

"You need your head reading," encouraged my friends. "He'll flatten you. You won't last a round!"

Commendably frank but not very good for morale.

In full agreement with them, since I had never stepped into a boxing ring in my life before, I advised them all to salvage something from the sorry affair by putting their money on Donald, and, whilst they were about it to put some of mine on him as well.

"You're not going to throw it?" accused Chonk as he took the money. Indignantly denying any such intention, I reassured him that there would be no need at all for that; it was a foregone conclusion anyway.

There was a full house in the gym when we stepped into the ring. Modest bets were laid everywhere and the odds I fear were astronomically against me. Donald's athletic prowess had ensured that.

He came dancing from his corner as the bell sounded. It was pretty to watch and I stood fascinated for a moment till uncomplimentary remarks from the spectators urged me to shamble to the middle. The dance continued round and round me, Donald's fists and head weaving and ducking in classic style.

It was really unfair because, totally unacquainted with the finer points of the sport, I brought up my dangling right fist from the region of my knee and hit him with it when he waltzed too close.

Straight under the chin it went. Donald's head snapped back sharply, his feet left the ground for a moment and, to my unbounded amazement, he lay recumbent with a very peaceful expression on his countenance. Neither of us had thought of the difference between boxing and fighting and I'd been brought up on the latter.

After a count of ten had failed to rouse the slumbering Donald, a wet cloth produced the desired effect and he was helped from the ring.

The bout was over in thirty seconds flat but, as usual, I found that I was a born loser. No-one loved me. I was nobody's hero. This was very understandable since most of my mates had lost money through me. I didn't even like myself very much, because I'd put money on Donald too.

Matters did not end there either. Donald insisted that I should join his boxing team for instruction, a pastime I found unduly boring and unprofitable.

After early childhood training in the 'backs' I was a natural for the rugger team. My knowledge of the game remained rudimentary to the end, but I was burly, had no inhibitions in the scrum and was generally useful against other colleges. Even so, my mediocre prowess seemed to bring nothing but grief.

We rashly accepted a challenge from an army team in an adjacent camp and should really have fled when we saw them advancing across the field. Compared to our hefty but youthful proportions they resembled nothing so much as the cast from a nature film shot in gorilla country.

We never knew why a ball was produced at all. They hurled us around the field like so many missiles. The only compensation for the loss of half of my proudly grown moustache was the magnificent hospitality they gave us afterwards. There was no return match.

Not long after this, the college ladies' hockey team challenged us to play them; at hockey of course. Gleefully we accepted and advanced onto the field full of confidence and ribaldry. After a sound thrashing and a fair time spent staunching the blood from the wounds on our notched shins, we challenged them to take us on at rugger. Very unsportingly they refused.

Our morale, never very high, soared after a rousingly successful match against an even worse team at Chester. Even so, they had the last word. This college possessed a magnificent old pavilion equipped with a fascinating set of toilet seats set in a row over a long galvanised trough. This flushed by means of a tidal wave, originating from a huge cistern at one end, and disappearing with a thunderous gurgle down a hole at the other.

Several of us, comfortably ensconced, should have suspected dirty work when one of the Chester team entered the cubicle at the cistern end. Only when the chain was pulled and a searing wall of flame from a floating mass of ignited newspaper fanned rapidly across our cringing posteriors did we realise that we had lost out again.

We did have a classical tribute to our ordeal. As the yells subsided, some wag from the Chester team solemnly declaimed from Milton's Paradise Lost, no doubt on their syllabus:

....as when the force
Of subterranean wind transports a hill
Torn from Pelorus or the shattered side
Of thundering Etna, whose combustible
And fuel'd entrails, thence conceiving fire,
Sublimed with mineral fury, aid the winds
And leave a singed bottom all involved
With stench and smoke.....

Two Birds and No Stones?

*L*ittle by little college became depleted as we enlisted in the armed forces. For the most part we left gladly. Of an age where more manly occupations held a greater attraction, the prospect of going back into school, even on the other side of the chalk as it were, had no great appeal for us.

Told to report to Catterick camp and stuffed with tales of the harsh discipline meted out by the army, I scraped together enough money to spend my last night before enlistment in the comfort of a Richmond hotel. It was a good move.

Free ale, I found, could be drunk all evening so long as one listened attentively to the somewhat dated advice from old sweats of the previous war.

The following morning, rather apprehensively, I reported to the guard room of the Royal Armoured Corps at Catterick. Amazed to see an eager rookie arriving in the morning instead of at the last permissible moment, a guide was detailed hastily to conduct me, like some honoured guest, to my future barrackroom.

Requested to wait for the arrival of my squad sergeant and meditating on the forbidding images of drill sergeants conjured up by the customary lurid tales of army life, I was mildly surprised to hear a kindly, soft spoken voice.

"By heck, lad. You're reet early!"

He was a middle aged gentleman wearing a smile like that of my father and the cap badge of an East Yorkshire regiment.

"I'd grab that bunk if I were you, lad. Well away from the door and late night drunks. No. The bottom one! You'll get draught from t'hopper up on top."

Fellow victims slowly began to report. All were received in the same paternal manner. Hitler's Wehrmacht would have stood aghast. We were a motley crew, ranging from a university professor to a little man from Leeds who insisted that he did nothing for a living except steal and fiddle. Despite his own advice that he be listed as a musician, on the strength of his fiddling, the gentle sergeant compromised by inscribing his civilian occupation as 'of independent means'! Pay books issued, our transformation into troopers had begun.

Army life at this period was pure Gilbert and Sullivan. We tore around receiving mostly useless training on obsolete equipment, protected and nursed like erring children by our military father figure, the parental squad sergeant. On one occasion, after fighting heath fires in the hills above the camp, there was real concern in his voice as he profusely apologised that we should march for two miles because of a transport failure. It was evidently not seemly that tank men should march!

By far the most frequent and efficient part of our training was ceremonial parade. Blanco-ed and shining, we could slow march, quick march and perform the most extraordinary rifle exercises to the beat of a drum like so many automatons. All this intensive military preparation must have lowered German morale no end. That, and the faultless efficiency which turned us out one night to hunt down parachuted German airmen with fifty rounds of .303 ammunition and rifles fitted with tubes to take only .22 bullets.

I suppose we could have hurled the rounds by hand.

Our training in marching, counter-marching and ceremonial

drill, worthy of a Guards Regiment at the trooping of the colours, was leavened by the real humour of certain of our superiors. The benevolent sergeant from the East Yorkshires, at the end of our first martial performance on the parade ground, turned his eyes heavenwards and fervently asked the Almighty what he had done to deserve the afflictions we imposed upon him. He followed up his prayer with a touching lament: "Oh mother, mother! Sell the pig and buy me out!"

His comments were bettered only by the Regimental Adjutant.

Each Sunday morning the whole regiment paraded on the square to display its skills in ceremonial marching and arms drill to the music of the unit's band. Before this warlike exhibition the Adjutant, followed by the squad sergeants, marched along the lines, front and rear, to inspect the 'turnout' of each individual trooper. He paused behind a soldier three men from where I stood rigidly to attention. The unfortunate man had forgotten to have his weekly haircut and his coiffure was at least two-thirds of an inch in length instead of the regulation quarter.

The Adjutant shouted: "Sergeant!"

"Sir!"

"Lift this man's hair aside in order that I may pass!"

The ranks quivered with mirth but stood fast, all except my neighbour who guffawed.

"Put that man on a charge along with Long Haired Lizzie! Conduct prejudicial to good order and military discipline!"

Highlights of this peaceful existence were the Sunday high teas that a small group of us had with a Quaker farming family in such an atmosphere of honest sincerity that even Slack, whose usual conversation would have brought a blush to the cheeks of a seventeenth century trooper, spoke like a curate in their presence. Not one of us looked at the four very pretty demure daughters with the normal lecherous appraisal in our eyes. There was no ulterior motive in the invitation they gave us. Not a word of pacifism or religion was spoken except for grace before meals.

Our idyllic military interlude at Catterick could well have been prolonged for a much longer period had any of us had the wit to fail our course examinations, thereby being set back again to square one. Human nature can be very strange. All of us worked much harder than we had ever done in our own vocations, even volunteering for extra morse practice and other useless bits of training; all in order to progress one more step towards posting, injury and, in all too many cases, death.

Thus after eight weeks the military honeymoon was over and we left for various tank units up and down the country. Along with two other theoretically trained tank men I reported to a Royal Tank Regiment at Crowborough, Sussex.

Our introduction was inauspicious. On preliminary Squadron O.C.'s interview, we leaped to heel-clicking attention in a manner that would have given credit to a guardsman and gave our names.

"Trooper Slack, Sir!"

"Trooper Tite, Sir!"

An incredulous irate bellow prevented any utterance from me.

"Are you trying to take the piss out of me, Trooper?"

Matters were not improved by my deplorable lack of soldierly restraint. I laughed, briefly but explosively. Unseemly and prejudicial to good order and military discipline! Obviously this intake was poor material for a fighting unit.

Verification of names made little difference to the distinct coolness that remained throughout the interview. After a few pungent comments on the shortcomings of our military decorum and the woeful inadequacy of our training as tank crew, we were detailed to our martial roles for the immediate future. This entailed slicing off the caked mud from the suspensions of the Valentine tanks with machetes, an operation universally known in the battalion as 'unterschitzenslizung.' Following this period of intense technical training in the cleansing of tracks and bogies, we were appointed as tank crew members barely knowing from which end of the guns the missiles emerged.

We greatly missed the gentle days of Catterick but there were odd spots of light relief such as the memorable occasion on which Tubby Wilson's tracked slave battery carrier slid down the icy road through camp, through the single bricked NAAFI wall and came to rest against the counter inside. Always placid, Tubby stuck out his head and asked the screaming waitresses for a 'char' and a 'wad.' We never heard the true text of the reply he received.

The first home leave from Crowborough was a huge success.

Tanks and crews were scarce at that early stage of the war and the Cambrai black beret and tank insignia still provoked considerable interest. We also carried a thirty-eight revolver in a thigh holster, strapped to the leg cowboy fashion with six spare rounds in loops on the holster. Despite disrespectful 'Howdy pardner!'s from other soldiers this went down very well with civilians, particularly of the opposite sex.

It was these six rounds that almost did for me. In the course of a much intertwined country 'walk' with my girl friend, she expressed the strange desire to try firing my revolver. Under the circumstances of the request refusal would have been unthinkable. I found a sheltered hollow, a very broad tree, loaded the gun and told her how to pull the trigger. She did this in rapid fire. The first shot went high on the hefty recoil, the other five progressively higher as her arm came up and over in an arc. The last one, by the sound of it, just cleared my head. When I'd finished shaking and putting the the gun away, she complained bitterly that her wrist hurt and that my immediate passion seemed to have cooled rapidly. Better than cold water, a near miss.

Back at camp, relationships with the fair sex were greatly limited by a firm and happy understanding with the girl at home who had almost shot me. In retrospect, I blush for the lost opportunities and the thoughts about me of the ladies concerned. Truly, I frequently left undone those things that ought to have been done and, though there was great health in me, chastity and faithfulness were frustrating in the extreme.

My knees were very quickly under the table of a hospitable family who were regularly visited by an exceedingly nubile and hot-eyed niece. Since her visits began to coincide with mine, a uniform and tank beret obviously served some purpose in the war effort.

Even at this distance in time I grow hot at the thought of all the hints I ignored, all the chances presented and I crawl with shame at recalling the night of the fire. We were all sitting comfortably indoors, each holding a glass of something and Cheryl trying hard to get a firm grip of my hand in the dusk.

It was just about time to put up the blackout screens when flames shot up a fair distance away in the direction of the camp.

"Come on," urged Cheryl, ever the opportunist, "Let's go and see it. Aunt and Uncle won't mind, will you?"

"Better not," said I. "I'll be nabbed for fire fighting."

The poor girl had not the slightest intention of going near the fire but she was game in more senses than one.

"Come on, then," she said grabbing my hand and pulling me to my feet, "Come on upstairs. We'll see it fine from the front bedroom window."

She hurried me upstairs, clasped my hand more firmly and, back to the window, leaned heavily upon me. Reddening with embarrassment at the recollection, I must confess to looking over her shoulder, trying hard to concentrate on the fire and wishing harder still that I was not so bloody faithful. After ten minutes or so the poor girl capitulated.

"Let's go down. Not up to much, is it?" she commented.

I'm not at all sure if it was the fire to which she referred.

Not many weeks passed before the battalion was due to be posted overseas. During that period I managed to obtain every type of leave known to the army with the exception of agricultural leave. Both my brothers were killed off for compassionate leave. Very touching were the letters they wrote describing each other's deaths for the benefit of my C.O.. Almost as good as the one I wrote describing my own for their benefit.

Finally we were all despatched on embarkation leave. Solemnly warned, a week before we went, to say not a word about our destination to a living soul, we were set to work, in full view of the road, painting our tanks a beautiful sandy yellow and fitting sand shields over the tracks. This top secret operation completed, we were issued with tropical khaki drill and paraded in it to ensure a reasonable fit. Maybe a fiendishly clever double bluff to convince the locals and any enemy agents that we were really off to Murmansk?

Off we departed for our last leave in Great Britain for five years, and back we came like so many sheep. It was on the last lap of this return journey that I shared a solitary compartment on the non-corridor train with a pretty little A.T.S. rookie. Around midnight the train was halted after pulling out of the station because of enemy bombing in the area. With no warning at all she burst into floods of tears. Nonplussed but ever gallant,

I gave her my handkerchief and asked what troubled her.

"I'm two days overdue from leave," she sobbed, "I stopped at home because my grandad came to see us."

"Cheer up," said Galahad. "Let's have a butcher's at your leave pass."

She came across to sit by me, fished it out of her side pocket and sobbed wetly all over my shoulder. I gave her a reassuring squeeze.

"Lean off a bit love and I'll fix it for you," said I, producing the standard kit for such emergencies. I inked an old indecipherable rubber stamp with my fountain pen, smearily thrust it on the pass and clinched matters with a touching confirmation of her grandfather's illness written above it and signed by six wiggles and a splodge, Sgt of Police.

She sighed heavily in relief, dried her tears and snuggled up closer in gratitude. Her arm slid round my waist and she smiled up at me in admiration, The train started off. I said nothing and did nothing. It was a slow short journey that lasted best part of an hour. As we pulled into Tunbridge Wells, she disengaged herself.

"It's a slow train," she said conversationally, "but everything seems very slow today."

I'm still troubled by this innuendo.

Tiny's Butterflies

*O*ur martial training in Britain never really convinced any of us of the great efficiency and dedication supposedly embodied in the armed forces. Despite the constant brainwashing we received to this effect it had been impossible not to observe that armed manoeuvres and even simple troop movements bore all the hallmarks, or perhaps it should be earmarks, of organisation by a cretinous six-year-old.

We were not therefore wholly surprised, when thrust into the Western Desert with the military training of a good Brownie troop, to discover that successes depended on either even greater inefficiency on the part of the enemy, or overwhelming numerical superiority on our own. Cynical by nature, we became increasingly sceptical when our own defeats invariably turned out to have been brilliantly planned feints and withdrawals masterminded by our infallible generals.

Not that we were so much better individually. The nearer the front line, the less we knew of either strategy or new developments. Tank crews knew least of all. Detailed knowledge of the front and of fresh enemy weapons seemed to be confined to the base wallahs in Cairo or Alexandria with time between their Birka or Sister Street bashing and imbibing to receive tuition in these matters. Certainly they regarded those sufficiently simple minded to be fighting up in the 'blue' with a justified contempt.

'Tiny' himself was not a base wallah in the true sense but, having had the good fortune to be seriously ill and sent to hospital in Cairo, he deviously prolonged his absence from sand and combat by means of innumerable courses and temporary relapses. Lacking the expertise of those permanently stationed in the delta he was finally winkled out and restored, protesting volubly, to our bosom.

Newly returned to the 'blue' from Abassia and the flesh pots of Cairo, Tiny lounged in the brief desert twilight, comfortably warming his considerable bulk against the stored heat of our tank's metal side.

Tiny held forth at great length. He was not a man of enormous rhetorical skill but, to those of us who had seen nothing but sand for months, his words were music.

The delights of courses held within a quick tank park stroll of the Birka stimulated an audience long deprived of the sight of even a female camel.

"Big, man? Like a bloody gorilla!" Tiny tastefully described his consort of a moment. "Hair on her belly like copper clock springs!"

He continued to outline her other endearing attributes in greater detail.

"More than a man could stand!" he concluded, and his audience groaned. Six months without leave in the delta, months of nothing but sand and soldiers, soldiers and sand, modified the outlook of the most fastidious amongst us.

Drooling mentally we urged Tiny to continue his saga of the delta hardships. Nothing loath, he squatted against the track and continued to tell his bedtime stories to a rapt audience.

Oily Pratt drifted over from the cook's wagon to take his place amongst the congregation. He sat down, idly fingering a small cylindrical canister from one end of which protruded a spindle, bearing wing-like projections.

"Found it out in the maidan," he volunteered. "Went out with me shovel and squatted right by it. Half buried in the sand."

His mate eyed it knowledgeably.

"It's Jerry," he said wisely. "Shufti the letters on it."

He took it from Oily's grasp.

"There's a screw thread on this spindle. If you twiddle the wings the screw goes in and out." So saying, he vigorously rotated the projections with his forefinger.

The attention of yet another esoteric Birka basher was diverted to Oily's find.

"Give us a butcher's then. It's not off a truck or anything like that. What do you reckon it's part of?"

Interest grew in the mysterious cylinder and it was passed from hand to hand for more detailed examination. Many were the speculations as to its origin and extremely diverse the peculiarly anatomical uses in which it was suggested Oily might employ it.

Little by little, the attention to Tiny's Cairene exploits waned and Oily's plaything was tossed from hand to hand round the circle. His captive audience lost, Tiny eased himself away from the track, preparatory to seeking more appreciative company, and was turning to go when his gaze fell upon the object which had stolen his thunder.

In all probability, the German Ninetieth Light, at no great distance from us, stood to for most of the night following the yell that issued from Tiny's throat. Certainly the whiskers of every gerboa as far as Tocra must have twitched in apprehension.

"Put it DOWN!" he bellowed. "Gently! Put it on the ground, gently, and run for it."

B Squadron tank crews froze for an instant before chortling a delighted appreciation of the big man's humour.

"Daft beggar! Frightened Oily half to death, blue lights and all! Burn the water tomorrow, he will."

Oily, thoroughly offended by the double slur on his courage and cooking ability, proposed a wholly impossible recommendation to Tiny and hurled the canister into the latter's massive fists.

Tiny's normally florid countenance abruptly lost colour. His speech, once he had regained it, did not. Tenderly laying the object at his feet he moved from its vicinity with a wholly uncharacteristic alacrity, trampling carelessly on those within his flight path.

"You shower of gits!" he shouted as he ran. "That's a Butterfly Bomb!"

This final gem of humour, butterflies and bombs in association, rocked his once more attentive audience who rolled about the sand in appreciation. Not often did such spontaneous entertainment occur in mid-desert.

Tiny stopped some distance away.

"Get away from it!" he wailed. "It's a booby bomb, I'm telling you. They'd got one at Abassia. Jerry drops them from aircraft all over the maidan. Those wings unscrew the rod and arm the bomb as it falls. It's only got to be touched to go off after that."

Mirth rose higher still. Always a joker, Tiny was indeed on form.

"Beggar off, Tiny. We've twiddled it in and out and thrown it around more than you did in the Birka! Pull the other one!"

So saying, Oily again picked up the canister. Tiny's spectacular sprint across the desert reduced all to side-shaking applause at his spirited performance and only Oily retained sufficient control to lob the canister after him.

When the splinters of shrapnel and dust had ceased to fall, our ears had stopped ringing and the crater viewed with some awe, Tiny gently pointed out that front line troops could not be expected to know owt about weapons. It took experienced base wallahs to know what was going on at the front.

Fear Naught!

*G*lory and heroics seldom came the way of seven troop. This always seemed grossly unfair since the happy accident of mechanical breakdown or simple loss of track on a modest sized landmine also never came our way. Always our tanks reached the battle area intact and, equally surely, some slapstick incident robbed us of all glamour without in the least impeding the disagreeable projectiles that gradually decimated our numbers.

Approach to the attack on the Mareth Line was by no means unpleasant. A peaceful daylight advance, with nothing worse than a mild strafing from the air, brought us safely to the waiting area of the spearhead forces due to attack at first light.

It was late afternoon when we halted and prepared a gourmet's meal of corned beef hash and biscuit 'burgoo.' We had finished the last of the tea when a Durham Light Infantry private drifted across to us. He cut short our apologies for the lack of tea to offer

GM admiring a daisy,
aged one

Uncle Harry, taken in Venezuela,
c1890, by a travelling photographer

The shantung shirt on GM aged
three – the 'Iron Bridge' era

GM in 1939 at the time of
the cycle trip to France

A

The convent at Crewe; site of brother Yanner's dalliance with a novice nun. The 'cannon' episode took place behind it.

Crewe Grammar School, now Ruskin Road School, has not altered in outward appearance, except for the road markings, since GM and Joan attended it.

Above: Joan – waiting for GM!.

Above: GM about 4 years after joining the 8th Army (Royal Tank Regiment)

Teatime in Sicily, after the ignominious retreat from the aged lady who chased us out of her tomato field.

C

All in Greece.
Above: thankful German prisoner after his desperate attempts to be captured. Below: Greek partisans. Above right: GM with two 'surrogate girlfriends'. Below right: on leave, strolling near Corinth, two weeks after the war had ended in Europe.

D

Left: GM as "rookie" soldier on last home leave before leaving Great Britain for four and a half years. Note the "Howdy Cowboy" tank man's revolver worn on the thigh.

Below left: GM photographed in Catania by a Sicilian photographer after the campaign was over and we were about to land on the Italian mainland.

Below right: GM in photo taken in Cairo just before landing in Greece

E

*GM pictured around the time of the trip with the
class into North Derbyshire*

Joan

*Passport photo of Joan aged
around 50.*

F

.Above: GM in France.

Left: Marriage at a moment's notice after years of separation

Below: Golden wedding celebrations in the Charente-Maritime.

Left: GM in France, now an honorary member of the Foreign Legion.

Below: the Morris home in Charente-Maritime.

with a query that left us momentarily bereft of speech.

"Wouldst like a drink then?."

We eyed him suspiciously. Drink? Real drink, way up the 'blue'?

"Pull the other then! It chimes mate."

"Nay lads," he replied. "Come with us. There's nowt only rum and gin but stacks of both."

We followed him sceptically across to his hole in the sand. He disappeared down wooden steps into an unbelievably spacious dugout. No miserable slit trench but an underground room, no doubt inherited from Jerry, revetted and ceilinged with wooden crate sections. Not a mere room either but Aladdin's cave stacked with supplies and, in pride of place, two crates each of rum and gin.

The Durham Light Infantry Regiment quartermaster sergeant, seated on one of them, raised his mug as we entered.

"Cheers!" he hiccoughed, "We dunna like drinking solo, lads. Get stuck in. It's thee birthday!"

It was indeed and we did get stuck in. Moses could not have found his manna more miraculous than we found our spirits in the desert.

I'm not too sure when we left the hospitable pair but the stars were out and the only light came from not too distant gun flashes and the occasional mortar flare. We experienced unusual difficulty in locating our tank but none at all in sleeping soundly which was odd since we woke at dawn lying in an uncovered heap by the track.

This strange encounter certainly caused a precedent as we made our dawn approach. Never before had we been wholly fearless in action, despite our regimental motto.

True, we cringed. Not from the enemy, however. From a hangover of monumental proportions. Every scrap of honest fright fled from us in the agony of clanking tracks and revving engines.

We felt real hate as never before. Not on account of the harmful objects an inconsiderate foe hurled at us, but for the obligation of returning his fire.

Each gun-slam was a self inflicted trauma and the red hot line of rivets, marching across the scalp at each burst from our own co-ax M.G., banished all fear of the Old Reaper.

Still agonising in post-alcoholic misery, it was only an error of judgment that averted our total destruction. Driver Glynn was displeased and gave his reasons in great detail. For our part, we felt that he was inconsiderate not to appreciate the difficulty of assessing accurately the position of the traversed turret in relation to the driving hatch, which was open at the time. Not to mention his lack of consideration for the pressure of nature's calls which necessitated emptying the shell case, containing the ample bladder contents of the turret crew, over the cupola edge. A mere quart or two descended upon him. Enough to cause him to miss his gear and roll us backwards downhill in time to avoid the hail of armour-piercing shells that virtually wiped out the rest of the squadron.

Glynn's prolonged and ungrateful description of the personal hygiene of the turret crew was interrupted by a very welcome call, on regimental frequency, to withdraw.

Hangover thrust aside, we hastened to comply. Jerry seemed to have a monopoly of missiles, dusk had fallen, the whole brigade was in confusion and our normal fear was fast returning. An additional radio warning of "Don't go down into the woods" seemed more apt to the Teddy Bears' Picnic. Since we took 'woods' to mean 'wadi' (a deeply cut dry stream bed down which water pours in torrents during rare downfalls of rain), across which lay our only line of retreat, we ignored the order.

Heroically hoping for a swift capture and resultant surety of existence as prisoners of war, we prepared to bale out at the first close contact of superior force. Hastily mustering suitably ingratiating phrases in German led, as usual, to the ridiculous. There was a difference of opinion amongst us as to the precise meaning of 'Nix Schiessen.' One school of thought held it to be 'Don't Shoot!' The other insisted it meant 'Don't empty your bowels!' General consensus decided that enemy reaction to the latter phrase might not be all that we desired and we determined to maintain a humble silence should the necessity arise.

Down we descended into the remains of the anti-tank ditch. Up the other side, and immediately up waist high from the turret, hands stretched aloft, as a determined horde of men swarmed onto the tank.

The anti-climax of a broad Geordie voice, telling us to get our ruddy hands down and drive us all out of this sanguinary shambles, typified all that ever happened to seven troop.

Not even permitted to surrender gracefully in battle, let alone distinguish ourselves!

Defeat

*O*ur initial part in the invasion of Sicily did very little for the reputation of B Squadron. On all other sectors there was fierce resistance to the landing of allied troops. Not so in our case.

We rumbled ashore from tank landing craft following a naval bombardment of the beach little short of a holocaust. For several hours the landing area had been subjected to shell and rocket fire almost worthy of Alamein and, when our tracks touched dry land, we were prepared for an equally devastating reply.

Turrets traversing frenziedly for targets, we ploughed up the beach to be met by two lonely German marines, hands held high and above, a bit shaken at being menaced by the combined fire power of two squadrons of heavy tanks. It was a truly heroic victory; two prisoners, the last of the defenders' rearguard left behind in error.

Much relieved and quite content with the lack of glory, we

swarmed off inland encountering no-one save the occasional Italian would-be prisoners of war.

They waved cheerfully to us as they passed by in the opposite direction seeking captivity, bully beef, security and peace.

It was a beautiful day. The sun shone, the countryside was green and fruitful compared to the arid desert we had left, and, best of all, no determined enemy threw hurtful missiles at us. We were truly happy. According to the friendly locals we consulted, Tedeschi had departed in good order some twenty-four hours ago. Expressing fervent hopes that his armour could travel faster than ourselves we continued our pursuit.

Troop by troop, line ahead, we penetrated deeper into former enemy territory. Mile by mile we became more relaxed. Progress differed only from Salisbury Plain manoeuvres in the complete lack of opposition and a casual approach to W/T procedure that would never have been tolerated during make-belief training.

A halt was called and we made tea, a troop at a time per squadron brewing up whilst the remaining tanks stayed on watch. There was a certain amount of reactionary levity as we sipped the diesel flavoured tea and basked appreciatively in the warm Sicilian sunshine, so relatively kind after the searing desert heat. The heavy gunfire we could hear in the distance both to left and right of us only emphasised the kindliness of fate in directing our landing to this sector.

As we sat, columns of lustily singing Italian soldiers, competently organising their own transfer to captivity, began to pass us and we felt just a little self-conscious at their cheery greetings. A complete rejection of warrior status and their knowledge of ensured future existence imparted an indefinable air of superiority which their dejected physical appearance could not conceal. No-one knew the Italian for 'mugs' but the word was implicit in their sympathetic looks and salutations.

Somewhat envious of our erstwhile enemies, we resumed the advance inland. There was still no sign of German opposition and by mid-day spirits ran high. Not a shot had been fired and the gunners complained that muzzle covers should have been left on to keep out the dust.

We halted at one o'clock to eat by the roadside. The fields of the nearby farm were well cultivated and green, lending the ambience of a country picnic to our meal despite the mass of armour still on alert. Diesel fires were lit to mash the tea and tins of bully beef prised open.

It was at this point that Davies of seven troop ventured to supplement his diet of hard tack with a ripe fruit or two from the adjacent tomato patch.

Long starved of any kind of fruit and mouths watering at the sight of it, the whole troop followed Davies' example. Busily picking away, we were caught literally red-handed when retribution fell upon us.

The shrill curses of the small, black-clad old lady hobbling rapidly across the field towards us, peeled away all the layers of Eighth Army toughness in an instant and we hastily retreated; invading soldiers on foray no longer but scrumping schoolboys caught in the act.

She pursued us all the way back to the tanks, shouting and waving her stick. We scrambled in out of her reach, started the engines and retired to the safety of four troop who made much of our discomfiture. The irate old lady had routed us where all of Mussolini's vaunted eight million bayonets had failed.

Our defeat and humiliation were not yet complete. Before we had resumed our interrupted meal the victorious old girl stumped across the field to us bearing a full basket of tomatoes.

Such magnanimity in victory so completed our own defeat that it was almost with relief that we soon made contact with the Hermann Goering Division, an enemy we could face on terms of equality.

Next To Godliness

nce the Sicilian campaign had ended and German forces were at a very pleasant distance away, across the Messina Straits, the entire regiment began to rejoice in a blissful period of enforced inactivity whilst awaiting replacements of men and tanks.

Our gear spread out widely amongst an expanse of gnarled old olive trees and we bivouacked on real grass with absolutely nothing to do except a minimal amount of tank maintenance, eat, sleep and line-shoot about the recent actions which had depleted our numbers. With no possibility of movement until essential supplies reached us, the whole situation became a soldier's paradise. True there was no feminine company to brighten our sex-starved existence but an abundance of local red vino compensated to a large degree and no-one grumbled.

This almost idyllic life in the olive groves was marred only by one small problem. There was an acute shortage of soap. We had none left and NAAFI supplies were non-existent. A certain standard of personal cleanliness could be achieved without the benefit of lather but the appearance of khaki drill uniform unwashed for weeks, save in plain water, lent the unit an air of social deprivation. Efforts to launder aertex undergarments in the mineral laden waters of Sicily were equally ineffective and pathetic grey 'smalls', dangling from the olive branches, gave the area a gypsy-like appearance. Not so much true gypsies, perhaps. I think they would have shunned us for lowering the tone of the neighbourhood. We more resembled down at heel tinkers fallen upon hard times. The regimental Sergeant Major, our high priest of spit and polish, was not at all a happy man.

The situation began to detract from our own contentment. Twelve hour periods of leave were due to be organised with transport into Catania and, even in occupied territory, a filthy uniform helped no squaddie to pursue his main interest in life and would certainly make the surrender of his quarry remotely unlikely. City pleasures became more remote with every day that passed.

The problem sorely vexed the Commanding Officer as well as we lesser mortals. Soap was needed. Leave was needed. Neither could be obtained without the other. Soap of a sort might be found in Catania but every official foray had failed to locate it. No doubt the base wallahs stationed in the city had now cornered the entire market and, by logical progression, the local talent as well. To discover any remaining soap obviously required strategy, incentive and deployment in strength.

All of these factors were contained in the announcement by the harrassed R.S.M..

One man from each troop, regardless of rank, was to be given leave to Catania on certain stringent conditions. He was to be as reasonably attired as our straitened circumstances permitted and he was to search diligently for soap. Thus each troop could find its own supply and salvation or leave would automatically cease as clothing progressively soiled. Incentive indeed! Our R.S.M. was nobody's fool.

Activity around the laager became frenzied. Seven troop pooled resources. Each man threw in the cleanest garment he possessed and all rubbed and scrubbed like men demented. In Catterick or

Bovington the result would have earned the wearer a lifetime of 'jankers', but we were proud of the effort. A valiant attempt, if not success, was evident. Arrayed in garments of various sizes and dubious cleanliness, I stood to be inspected by the other members of the troop.

Comradely comments, always candid and seldom encouraging, varied from comparisons with Coco to downright scurrilous aspersions. Thus encouraged, I presented myself to Headquarters for official inspection.

Much relieved to find that the motley gathering of ill-clad soldiery consisted of my would-be fellow travellers, I fell in beside them. As the sergeant major inspected us I think we all felt as sorry as one can feel for a W.O.1. He drooped visibly and concluded the dismal ceremony with a minimum of delay.

"In normal times," he moaned, "I would not pass you for a coal fatigue party. Get in the truck out of my sight and for God's sake find some soap!"

An hour of ribald song brought us into Catania and heaving ourselves from the waggon we dispersed with the rapidity of released homing pigeons. Each had his own priority of needs in mind but the true object of the quest was not forgotten. Future leave depended on success.

Two or three quick vinos to fortify us and the search began. The quest for the Holy Grail must have been child's play in comparison.

"Sapone," I was curtly informed, "Tutti finito!" "Soap all gone." Shop after shop, laundress after laundress. No soap to be had for money and certainly not for love in a city where that commodity was readily available and cheap.

Determination began to flag by noon and inquiries were interspersed with periods of refreshment. The larger the latter the less pressing seemed our objective and it was a little hazily that I read the notice in the shop window against which I leaned for temporary support.

"Poudra Sapone," it read. "Soap Powder." Soap Powder!

Beneath the notice lay a heap of dirty white granules. Two kilos of the stuff I bought at a price which cast some doubt as to the real victors in Sicily.

The rest of the afternoon and the journey back are of no significance. Suffice it that I entered camp grinning through an alcoholic haze and clutching the precious bundle to my chest. My welcome was tumultuous. Never have I been so popular.

Gallons of water were poured into the dhobi tin, a generous double handful of powder added, and the mixture set to stew over a blazing diesel fire. Whilst it heated we stripped to the skin and, filled with the pride of achievement, I thrust the clothing deep into the water. I stirred as the scummy mixture boiled and the wholesome odour of washday wafted around us. A mere ten minutes and the cloth seen at the surface of the murky liquid was clean beyond belief. Everything appeared to be of a whiteness beating the most optimistic soap advertisement, even the drill uniform which should have remained khaki.

Master of ceremonies, I took up the pot stick and one by one, unfortunately piece by piece, lifted out the spotless snow white garments. They called to mind the dressmaking patterns we had seen at home. Not garments but the components thereof. Here a sleeve piece, there a collar as it were. Cloth remained but of stitches not a trace. All had gone.

My conciliatory remark that everything was there, clean if not coherent, was not kindly received and the derogatory comments about my soap-seeking abilities were unstinted and personal. Recriminations continued during our march across the camp, in a state of nature, bearing our clean disintegrated offerings towards the Quartermaster's truck. The incredulity on his cynical face at the sight of our pitiful fragments diverted further comment from me. A speechless Quartermaster at last! No possible refusals. Complete new gear or a stark naked seven troop.

As I virtuously pointed out afterwards, the victory was mine, the desired result achieved. Spotless raiment for all in less time than one could dry a shirt.

Sea-food For Thought

S uccessful inter-services co-operation, we were told, depended upon mutual trust and understanding. Within our own services there was certainly a very clear and very suspicious understanding, no trust at all and a somewhat shaky co-operation. The co-operation was always willing enough but, with few exceptions terminated in disorganised chaos.

For some time after the breakthrough at El Alamein, the Mediterranean Sea remained very much an Axis lake. Consequently, lines of communication and supply across the desert elongated to such an extent that our own armoured brigade ground to a halt, close to Buerat, because of fuel shortage.

This situation was relieved by the dispatch from the delta of a Tank Landing Ship packed solidly with diesel and petrol fuel, contained in forty-four gallon drums and jerricans.

The entire operation depended for success upon a high degree of co-operation involving the navy, a company of engineers, our own tank personnel and a labour force of Mauritian pioneers, all working together in a vast do-it-yourself scheme to offload our immediate supplies.

We marvelled open-mouthed at the speed with which the sappers deftly built an intricate scaffolding jetty far out into reasonably deep water and noted, with great approval, that a roller goods conveyor was already in process of installation along the top of it. We should only need to station ourselves at intervals along it and accelerate the drums and cans in the direction of the next man along the line. Very thoughtful of the sappers. The only humping to be done was on the beach and that could be left to the Mauritians.

In due course the flat-bottomed tank landing ship arrived, dropped a stern anchor for hauling off again, and sailed towards the newly built jetty. On she came, with magnificent verve and style, to completely demolish the end of the jetty and topple the remainder into the sea.

Slowly withdrawing from earshot of the colourful descriptions of sailors' habits and abilities, in general and particular, bellowed by the considerably displeased sappers, the tank landing ship lay offshore thoughtfully for an hour or so.

As always, when in doubt, we took the essentials of British warfare from the tank and made tea whilst external problems resolved themselves. We had just concluded our refreshment when the ship came in again, at a fair clip, to beach in the ordinary manner for such craft. Probably due to excessive loading, she beached in water far too deep for anyone to reach her lowered ramp in less than chest-high water. This appealed to no-one ashore and our O.C. refused point blank to use his men under such conditions. His own suggestion was reluctantly taken up by the Navy and the services of seven troop were demanded.

A thick hawser was run ashore from the beached landing ship and the towing wires of our three tanks shackled to the eye of it. With a naval officer to call the tune we all engaged first gear, took the strain, and crept up the beach with the L.S.T. in tow. Concerned by the sailor's gestures and unable to hear his voice above the engine noise, we made greater efforts and pulled harder still.

It was only when a jeep raced across the front of us that we realised he had been frantically urging us to stop, and I quote, "before the fornicating ship reached the next bloodstained oasis."

Thanks to our enlightened self help, unloading proved to be very easy. We hardly wet our feet. By evening the L.S.T. was empty, our tanks were full, the transport trucks loaded with fuel and we departed together. All, that is, except the beached landing ship. She was still vainly churning astern and winching desperately on her stern anchor when we disappeared over the horizon. Probably she is still there as a monument to inter-services co-operation.

Thoughts of this North African interlude were in our minds as we waited to board the L.S.T due to carry us from Sicily to the Italian mainland. There was little love lost between the British Navy and ourselves on such operations. Tanks were marshalled in the hold of a Tank Landing Ship with the cold efficiency of the silent service. Matelots watched every move of the tank crews with all the vigilance of a butler whose master has declared open house to the district's tramps. No supervising sailor ever left the hold before the last soldier was safely top-side and the bow doors closed. Hatches were secured and locked. Not primarily against the sea.

An L.S.T. operating far from base carried a bulk supply of rations in the after part of the tank deck, and rations to a tank man were as lodestone to a magnet. He had the appetite, his vehicle had the carrying capacity and his rapacity was well known to the Royal Navy. Understanding in plenty but no trust of any sort, whatever the degree of co-operation.

Because of this mutual understanding between our two services, we were overjoyed to see the Stars and Stripes flying on the L.S.T. approaching our quayside. She docked and we awaited the usual detailed and precise instructions for our embarkation.

At length, a rating sauntered out of the bow, approached the C.O., shifted his gum to one cheek and queried: "What you guys waiting for? Roll 'em in: the front door's open."

Somewhat taken aback by this casual approach, we rolled 'em in. No-one watched. We shackled down the tanks and left the hold.

A little later, the marked absence of soldiers on deck indicated that those remaining were missing out on something. We dived below. The sleeping quarters were equally deserted. Then we saw the hatches. Unlocked and fastened open.

The buzz of great activity sounded from below. We approached and looked. If one places a pile of sugar by an anthill and marvels at the speed and activity involved in its removal, an idea can be gained of the scene in the hold, except that ants are sluggards by comparison. The tank deck seethed with khaki forms.

From tank to tank they leaped, disappearing occasionally to deposit their loads, re-emerging to return for more. Cases were borne on shoulders, tins were hurled from hand to hand. Aladdin's cave in the after part of the hold became Mother Hubbard's cupboard in a matter of minutes. The locusts had been.

Disembarkation at Manfredonia, the following morning, was without incident. No check had been made by our trusting allies. The squadron rolled a few miles down the coast to a temporary camp. Tanks were spaced along by the sea with a skill and precision marred only by the incredulous exclamations of the locals as crew after crew depressed the 75mm gun, removed the muzzle cover, and deftly caught the tins of milk as they cascaded therefrom. Our martial image, I felt, was more than a little tarnished by this chocolate soldier episode. Not at all in line with the concept of armoured might left by the Panzer regiments we were displacing.

At dusk a worried O.C. toured the squadron in person.

"Get rid of the lot, lads!" he said. "We've been rumbled. Official search tomorrow!"

Operation Acquisition swung full speed into reverse. The darkness became alive with scurrying forms bearing bundles. Within thirty minutes not a can remained in the area.

Morning brought the promised inspection. It was martial enough to dispel any local doubts of our soldierly behaviour. Heels thudded, salutes were thrown, Top Brass inspected and questioned as Brigade H.Q. sergeants searched the tanks.

Not a can, not a label was discovered. Injured innocence shone from all our faces. The searching sergeants muttered disbelieving oaths as our O.C. graciously accepted the grudging apologies offered.

The native populace were deeply impressed by the disciplined efficiency of our inspection and regarded us with a new found respect. This performance had been more in line with our German predecessors.

It seemed a great pity that two hours later they should witness a squadron of bare-legged tank men paddling in the sea and stooping from time to time to gather cans from the sea bed.

The Fifth Deadly Sin

The tank man on active service was something of a Cinderella. His pickings were ever meagre. Remote and encapsulated in our iron monster, we ground past all the unconsidered trifles which the infantry snapped up in passing as a child picks wild flowers. Not that we wished to loot, I hasten to add, but merely to 'liberate' a few creature comforts. A little fresh food, some fruit or a bottle or two. By the time we could halt and return, the cupboard was always bare.

Thus it was that, during a rare period of rest, seven troop, bearing surplus boots, blankets and all convertible commodities not actually welded down, sought out the local farms. Italian peasants were rarely loath to barter profitably and before long the troop area rapidly began to resemble something between a military harvest festival and a county agricultural show. Baskets of apples, figs, potatoes and all manner of farm produce lay stacked against the tracks.

A vociferously protesting turkey was tethered on a long cord to a towing shackle but our duck was free to roam. It was no waddling stupid Aylesbury, this one, but a veritable peacock, proudly parading her iridescent colours and noisily following us around.

Feasting day planned, the fattening process began. Both birds ate heartily, the turkey with an air of grudging complaint and the duck endearingly from our hands. The latter, indeed, followed us around like a pet for much of the time remaining to her.

Our main course did not materialise until the day before the banquets when we located a sucking pig. It was the runt of the litter and not much use to the farmer but plump enough for us and well worth my old battledress trousers. Back at camp and dumped squealing from the sack, he turned his beady eyes suspiciously upon us and fled, hotly pursued through the squadron lines in a Dickensian hue and cry. His capture and subsequent incarceration in the tank blanket box ensured a restless night for us all as he snuffled and thumped his way ceaselessly around the metal confines, disdaining the straw bed we had laid in it.

A certain cowardly diffidence marked our approach to preparations for the meal. All of us were well acquainted with food on the hoof. All had handled it oven ready, but no-one could view with equanimity the process of transition from the former state to the latter. Well hardened to the extermination of our own species, we blenched at our present problem. Turkey and pig had inspired little affection, such is the effect of over-protestation, but duck had eaten from all our hands and even now stood by our feet, head cocked expectantly on one side in case a crumb or two should fall her way.

Goliath Jones, five feet two of farmer's son, graphically described the alleged rapid and humane killing of a large turkey. Apparently one stood upon its feet and, with the bird stretched behind the back, one pulled the poor creature's neck sharply over the shoulder, thus snapping the neck immediately. Our cries of incredulous derision provoked him into offering his services.

In a flurry of feathers and a cacophony of gobbles and curses, Goliath and turkey took their respective stances. Whitey quickly laid odds on the turkey as Goliath's spine began to arch backwards. Something had to give. It was Goliath's grip. Gobbling triumphantly, turkey made for the wide open spaces and Goliath fell flat on his back to the resounding cheers of all the squadron. Turkey was most definitely off the menu. We never saw him again.

Two more reluctant executioners were decided by lottery. In spite of all the chicanery we could muster, Whitey and I drew the short straws. Whitey revolted at the idea of pigsticking and refused to despatch his victim with anything smaller or less humane than a .45 slug from his Thompson sub-machine gun. Given unrestricted choice, I think he would have held its head against the muzzle of the 75mm with an A.P. up the spout. Anyway, in his agitation and anxiety for a clean kill, he forgot to set the gun at single shot and blew off most of the piglet's head, and almost his own foot, with the ensuing burst of rapid fire.

Eviscerated, crammed with tomato, biscuit and onion stuffing and sewn up ornamentally by Slack, an upholsterer by trade, pig was laid to rest in the ammunition box oven.

After much deliberation I chose a machete to deal with duck.

It would be quick and sure I argued. Chop the head clean off and quickly turn away. Davies and Chalky were reluctantly persuaded to stretch duck upon the block. Chalky who held the head end apprehensively exhorted me,

"For Pete's sake remember it's the neck you're supposed to hit, not my wrist!" In view of my nervous determination, I felt considerable sympathy with his lack of faith in my accuracy. In the event I managed not to amputate his hand, but anxiety to finish duck cleanly lent me such strength that it took two of us to prise the machete from the log beneath my victim's neck.

Once despatched, prepared and cooking merrily, the pathetic corpses ceased to worry us as the savoury odours drifted across the laager. We dined like princes on their richly browned carcasses and the flagons of chianti in which we toasted their departure. Replete and eructating contentment, we staggered to the shade of an olive clump and blissfully snored.

Alas for all transgressors of the fifth deadly sin! Within the hour our victims rose to seek retribution. They rose literally, or, as Whitey put it, we were all proper poorly.

Weary and spent, we gathered our blankets from the box and

settled for the night. But not for long. We itched. We scratched. We shook our blankets and fought all night a losing battle against the post mortem porcine vengeance. Fleas! Aggressive fleas, hungry fleas. Deprived of their normal diet, left pigless in the blanket box, they made a hearty meal of us.

Morning could not come too soon. Pig had triumphed over death. The only full-bellied were his fleas. The legacy of livestock that he left kept us company for some time. His fleas gaily hopped about the turret for days. They leaped from breech block to radio, from gunner to loader and back to commander, emphasising his victory with every bite. Pig was avenged.

For What We Have Received...

S omewhat impeded by a pound or so of scrap iron lodged in me, I baled out of our blazing tank without standing upon the ceremony of my departure. Rolling as far from it as I was able, I waited in abject terror for someone to come out for me.

It was near Lanciano and seven troop had given a fair bashing to the entrenched German infantry until they whistled up their own tanks. They were Panthers, a superior tank to ours, and the first to appear had a faster and better gunner than we did. He put an A.P. shell from his 75 mm Special straight into us, on the track line, transforming the turret into a buzzing hive of hurtling fragments and flame. It was no place to linger unnecessarily.

I'd lain shivering for quite a while before a certain jubilation intruded into the shock of wounds and concussion. I was alive and that was good. Furthermore I was in bad shape, a 'Blighty one' for sure, a ticket for home booked and paid for! Nothing ludicrous about this one either. Honest battle wounds. Glamour and heroics at last! About time too. My last wounding had been at the Marethe Line fiasco, not in the heat of attack but safely retreating from the whole colossal blunder. Sitting in the turret, rejoicing in escape to unexpected safety, I had collected a hail of shrapnel from a stray 88 mm air-burst low over the tank. Injury and slapstick as usual. A kick in the pants on leaving the party.

These incoherent semi-conscious thoughts were interrupted by the arrival of stretcher bearers, which was just as well since the tank, by then, was giving a fair imitation of a 'Brock's Benefit' far too close to be comfortable.

After being carried to comparative shelter I began to laugh weakly.

"Poor bugger's hysterical," one R.A.M.C. chap remarked to the other as they loaded me into the ambulance. I hadn't the strength left to tell him that I'd just realised my wounds were all in the back. No glamorous scars to display, only ugly evidence of apparent flight from the enemy. Things were back to normal.

All the kicks and no ha'pennies. Quite comforting in a perverse sort of way.

Safe in the ambulance, I made a second acquaintance with the Society of Friends. The vehicle had been provided and manned by the Quakers. These boys were the conscientious objectors to warfare that our own brave base wallahs termed cowards, operating up among the tanks with no protection at all; the bravest men I ever saw. They could not have been more relaxed and calm if they had been driving down an English country lane.

Through the sausage machine of Casualty Clearing Stations and operated upon in a field hospital, I achieved the ultimate, a berth on the hospital train to Taranto for embarkation on a hospital ship to England. The German on the berth above me had also been wounded before at Marethe and we reminisced about our various common experiences, including the huge wave of surrendering Italians who had come over to us at the start of the action. He was something of a philosophic wit, this fellow.

"It's only fair," he said dryly in excellent English, "You were stuck with the blighters in the last war. We've got them this time."

It was all too good to be true. A few hours en route for home and I was seized by increasingly severe rigors. I found difficulty in moving my neck muscles and began to arch up on my head and heels. The R.A.M.C. orderly who spotted my condition returned with the Medical Officer. He examined me briefly, consulted my pay book for the last date of anti-tetanus injection, and gave instructions for me to be off-loaded at Bari and taken urgently to the General Hospital there.

Shot full of anti-tetanus serum and stuck on a drip feed of the same, I hovered in a vague and painful twilight before deciding there were still things to do in this world and beginning to suck on my feeding cup. Nursed during a couple of months back to a semblance of health, the necessity to repatriate me for further hospital treatment had gone. As usual, things ended in a whimper, not a bang.

Flying from Bari to Catania hospital in a D.C.3 was full of interest. Easing up from the stretcher, I could just see from a window. We seemed to be at nil altitude and almost clipping the wave tops.

"Yeah Mac," volunteered one of the American crew. "We got no red cross markings. It's you guys down and munitions back up. We hug the coast right low to keep out of sight of Kraut fighters." Very intriguing but not so reassuring.

Graduated from hospital to convalescent camp and finally discharged to transit camp, I joined hordes of assorted personnel all waiting to be returned to their respective units. My own regiment seemed to have vanished without trace until I encountered one of the rear party on brief shore leave from a liberty ship that had put into Catania. During my absence the regiment had been withdrawn and sent to Egypt. Hastily grabbing what little kit I possessed and bidding the transit camp a soldier's farewell, I joined the rear party and sailed for Egypt.

Docking at Malta en route to Alexandria, we were privileged to experience the evening's entertainment of a lifetime. Just before we entered the Grand Harbour at Valetta, an American cruiser and a British destroyer, both desperately manoeuvring among the mass of wrecked shipping, collided with each other. By some freak of impact the bows of the much larger and heavier American ship sustained severe damage whilst the British destroyer escaped virtually scot-free.

That evening, liberty boats from both ships put ashore with substantial numbers of matelots all heading, like ourselves, for the mundane delights of the 'Gut'.

With true British tact, the men from the destroyer made a point of remarking upon the tin-can flimsiness of U.S.N. cruisers to any American ratings they encountered. Full of beer and high spirits, the two sides joined in battle, gathering reinforcements from any of their seagoing nationals as the fight progressed.

As neutral swaddies, we stood and watched delightedly as the naval battle rolled back and forth along the 'Gut'. All differences of opinion instantly ceased when the naval police appeared on the scene and British and American matelots stood shoulder to shoulder against the common enemy. Since some two hundred or more combatants were involved it took some time before the police had matters in hand and the entertainment was concluded.

The police departed with those too drunk to escape and a mixed batch of ex-combatants surged into our bar, flushed with beer, fight and triumphant escape from authority. They took us under their wings and, calling loudly for more beer, settled down to celebrate their former hostilities.

At something like one o'clock in the morning my companions and I found ourselves teetering at the edge of the quayside and peering owlishly at the long pontoon bridge spanning the oil-covered filthy water that lay between our ship and dry land. It was only two feet wide and oscillated alarmingly underfoot, as we had found on coming ashore.

Full of Dutch courage, voices raised in discordant song, we stepped out boldly. Gaining confidence at every step, we ran; we capered; we jumped up and down to show our expertise, and I fell into the noisome depths.

Fuel oil and rotting debris of unmentionable varieties clung about me as my companions heaved me back onto the causeway. Their merriment increased in proportion to the growing lyricism of my verbal appraisal of the Grand Harbour and its contents. I squelched an odorous way back on board, the only sober one amongst us. Better than black coffee that sudden baptism. An innocent victim of international disagreement.

Six days later I rejoined the regiment in Egypt to find them tank-less and unhappily playing soldiers with rifles and other weird infantry impedimenta. Apparently this was to be a rest for us, a reward for prolonged active service. We were to have the honour of first landing in Greece the moment the Germans showed any signs of withdrawal. Since tanks were deemed to be of little use in the operation and, we suspected, no transport available for them, we were temporarily to become infantrymen. We were terrified and horror stricken.

In due course our ship entered Piraeus Harbour and to our unbounded relief we saw the last of the German rearguard trucks hightailing it away in the hills beyond. Heroes once more, we marched towards Athens garlanded like victors by the enthusiastic Greeks.

"Long live Churchill!" they shouted. "Long live Roosevelt!"

They seemed rather puzzled by our recommendations as to what could be done with both these dignitaries.

Fear The Greeks

*L*ife in Greece promised to be full of interesting variety. To begin with we were billeted in the Zappion building close to a large wooded park and not too far from the city centre.

With nothing to do except fraternise with the locals, the time passed very pleasantly. Each evening the park seethed with activity. It proved to have been the main stamping ground of Athenian ladies of the town during the German occupation. A change of uniform meant nothing to these hard-working girls.

All was grist that came to the mill and they did not lack for custom amongst the ranks of a regiment already several years away from home.

Many of these ladies acquired new names amongst the aficionados. A rather slant-eyed beauty soon answered to the title of Eskimo Nell, Miss Muffet carried her own little cushion with her, but why Nelson was so called and how Virgin Mary earned her unlikely sobriquet beggars imagination.

One or two of the girls quite enjoyed chatting with a non-client during their rest periods and their conversation, conducted in a lingua franca of Greek, Italian, German and English, was always interesting and often very enlightening. Their trade was fiercely competitive and seemed, in the light of later experience, to be the most active Athenian business.

It was not long before our masters whisked us away from the sybaritic existence at the Zappion to Goudhi, an outlying suburb of Athens. Here we settled into an ex-German barracks far too big for our small force and surrounded by high barbed wire. The reason for this became obvious when some five hundred, brutally ill-used, German and Italian prisoners were marched in by a shambling crowd of Greek partisans all resembling Wild Bill Hickock, if one can imagine that character steeped in garlic and draped around with belts of machine-gun rounds.

Obviously we were now to be re-cast as P.O.W. guards. The task proved to be very restful and even entertaining at times. Seven troop had the responsibility of guarding a two-storey block of prisoners; not a very onerous duty since the last place they wished to be was outside the barbed wire, beyond which they relied on us, as their guardian angels, to keep the Greeks at bay.

The ground floor was occupied by Italians, the upper by Germans, an arrangement that soon developed into a situation in the realms of comic opera. Access to the toilets of this block was conveniently situated on a landing between the two floors, and we became extremely puzzled to observe the whole of the Italian contingent urinating, and worse, outside the building.

When we remonstrated with the offenders they shrugged their shoulders, hurled their hands around and demanded, in the names of their mothers and the Mother of God, what else they could do with a German guard permanently posted outside the toilets, denying them their natural rights.

Marching briskly through the shouting, gesticulating crowd, a deputation of Germans arrived, stamped to attention before us, saluted smartly and very formally demanded why they should be subjected to the indignity, bordering on atrocity we gathered, of being housed with Italians.

"Ve haf closed to them the abort," their spokesman solemnly

explained. "Out they vill go or burst their vorkings!"

The German contingent still stood in puzzled and slightly disapproving aloofness when we had finished rolling around in uncontrollable merriment and begun to arrange an exchange of our Italians for a batch of Jerries from eight troop.

During this Ruritanian interlude, a weary figure appeared at the main entrance pathetically waving a German paybook at the guard and pleading to be admitted to the delights of our holiday camp. Since he was clad in a British battledress blouse and a pair of khaki shorts, speaking impeccable upper class English and using all our Eighth Army colloquialisms, he was given short shrift.

"Bugger off, mate. We've got enough nutters in here without English comedians as well. Go and take the piss out of some other unit."

The rejected supplicant departed, only to return when there was a change of guard. This time he waved his paybook, leaped to Teutonic attention, shouted his name, rank and number in German and refuted all knowledge of the English language. Only after he had been admitted, searched and listed did he revert to his officers' mess English.

"Thank God you've let me in," the poor chap said. "I've been wandering round Athens for two days hiding my nationality from the Greeks and trying to give myself up to every British swaddie I met. Every bloody one told me to get lost and play the fool somewhere else."

He had been born in Greece of German parents and had obviously been left behind after being schooled in Eighth Army slang as part of German Intelligence. He had decided that there was no future in this and was desperate to be taken in as a ordinary P.O.W. and not as a spy.

We fed our happy prisoner who had not eaten for forty-eight hours. Safely incarcerated, secure from Greek lynchings and eating again, he could not thank us enough for the floor space, palliasse and two blankets with which he was issued. Wilhelm's gratitude took a practical turn as well, in the form of infallibly sound advice on where to go in Athens for good entertainment of whatever nature was desired.

Life at Goudhi was good and, like everyone else, I soon had my knees firmly beneath a Greek table. There were two extremely attractive girls in the household, Poppi and Dina, with whom it was very pleasant to spend the odd hour or so, even if well chaperoned.

The first threat to this peaceful life came in the form of bundles of posters and pots of paste. E.L.A.S. partisans had so far refused to lay down their arms and wandered about the streets armed to the teeth in defiance of all Scobie's requests for disarmament. Now we had the dubious honour of posting up an ultimatum to all guerrillas to hand in their arms within twenty-four hours. We did this billsticking in unarmed parties of four, surrounded by derisive groups of partisans convulsed with mirth as they read our notices. They had some justification since they outnumbered us by some thirty to one.

We returned to Goudhi and the welcome barbed wire with something of the pleasure Wilhelm had experienced. The Germans found it difficult to conceal their amusement as the twenty-four hours drew to a close with the sounds of scattered shooting down in Athens. After all, they had already predicted this outcome to us on our first acquaintance. They also offered to join in the defence of the camp if we would arm them, giving their word that all weapons would be returned once the danger was over. This was an offer we found eminently sensible but which higher authority refused to countenance.

Around midnight, seven troop with the rest of B Squadron was abruptly roused, loaded onto three-ton trucks and transported at breakneck speed back to the Zappion in Athens. Sporadic shooting could be heard from all over the city and we learned to our unbounded dismay that we were to attack the partisan headquarters the following morning, infantry fashion.

Next day, the truck conveying seven troop to battle failed to reach its objective. Halfway through the park, a burst of tracer crackled across the canvas hood, and the sledge hammer blows of heavy machine gun rounds, whipping through the metal sides, sent us hurtling over the tailboard like so many trampoline artists.

We ran across the park faster than Olympian sprinters. Whooping and breathless, deeply regretting our intake of alcohol since arrival in Greece, Connah and I reached the broad road across which lay the Zappion from which we had emerged half an hour earlier. Dismayed by the odd bullet which ricocheted from the road at intervals, Connah voiced our common thoughts.

"I'm buggered if I can run another bloody step," he gasped. "Let's go together, wide spaced and jinking."

We did. Whether the marksmen were put off by the sight of us apparently doing turkey trots and funny walks, I don't know, but every shot went wide and, safe in the porchway, we hammered for admission.

The other two truck loads were already back. They had returned at speeds more appropriate to Monza after seeing our truck go up in smoke.

Once more we set out, this time on foot and by devious ways across the Palace gardens where an observer would have been vastly intrigued to see us rolling on our backs in any filth we could find like so many itching horses. The fact is that our webbing was snow white, beautiful for mounting guard and guaranteed to delight any marksman who put his sights upon us. By the time we emerged from the gardens our splendour had been suitably dulled and, very scruffy but much happier, we reached the assembly point for our attack.

To add insult to injury, we found a tank facing our objective ready to smash down the entrance door and grill so that we could run howling like maniacs up the stairs for our baptism in house fighting. We made it to the top and shot or captured all those too slow to leg it away across the roof tops. George Shaw and McBlane distinguished themselves by hammering on opposite sides of the same door with their tommy gun butts, bellowing to each other to come out and firing bursts through it at the supposed enemy on the other side, fortunately with no success.

With one casualty dead, we withdrew to allow a company of newly arrived paratroops take over the empty building.

Our fortunes ran true to form. We found that A Squadron had been equipped with ancient tanks rushed over from Italy. Tatty old Shermans, no longer fit for much, but still tanks. There were not enough for us and we did not receive our geriatric tanks until we'd suffered further infantry style sorties.

The crowning insult to our efforts came weeks later when Connah received a newspaper from home with a full front page picture of us charging into the partisan headquarters under the caption of "The Paratroopers Do It Again!"

Perhaps we should not have told the news reporter where to go and what to do with his camera before we made our attack.

Reprieve

The tanks we had been promised failed to materialise until after seven troop had made several more sorties as infantry. Very reluctant heroes, we were delighted to see increasing numbers of real foot soldiers arriving who really knew what they were about at ground level.

Our last attack in the guise of P.B.I. resulted from a disastrous error in weapon handling by a member of eight troop. They had been ordered to attack and occupy a large three-storey building, an apartment house whose frontage commanded the length of a street still largely occupied by the partisans.

In the course of checking guns, ammunition and so forth, eight troop primed and placed its supply of thirty-six type grenades and a few phosphorous bombs on a large table in the Zappion room they occupied. One of their number primed the last of his own grenades with a four second detonator, screwed up the base plug, pulled out the pin in a moment of mental aberration instead of splaying out its ends safely, and placed it alongside the others.

A less dozy trooper saw the lever fly off, heard the initial crack of the detonator and bellowed anguishedly:

"GET DOWN! ON THE FLOOR!"

But for his quick wits eight troop undoubtedly would have been wiped out. As it was, the massive table directed most of the blast and shrapnel upwards or outwards and, though everyone received a share, there were no fatalities.

After eight troop had been carried or helped into ambulances, we were ordered to replace them in the attack.

Unhappily we made our way across the city, sidling along the pavements against the walls, covering one another from doorway to doorway and across intersections. It intrigued us above a little, as we neared our objective, to pass genuine infantry crouched down against the walls. Why, as mere amateurs at this particular game, we should be leapfrogging beyond them to carry out the attack we could not imagine. Perhaps bureaucracy had forgotten that we were tank men.

Covering the last few yards at a furious run, we burst in the door and scattered through the building yelling ferociously and calling on the enemy to surrender. The place was deserted. Not unnaturally, no-one felt at all disappointed about this and we set about organising ourselves into defensive positions at all the windows.

Our weapons installed at all vantage points covering the street, we had begun to relax a little when someone on the top floor heard suspicious noises of movement from overhead. Investigation revealed a door opening onto attic stairs.

Once again a party leaped up the stairs bellowing a ferocity they did not feel.

This time they were out-howled by the hysterical screaming from above. Out of the attic poured a dozen or so young women, all more or less nubile and attractive followed by a battered old harridan of uncertain age who shepherded them to the lower level.

Dumbstruck with amazement we listened to her explanation, given in an all but incomprehensible transatlantic English. It was fluent New York, and Bowery at that.

"We toit youse guys wus E.L.A.S. on a screw and kill jag. I had de goils up dere two days awready."

Proudly the old battleaxe informed us that she had been an 'acrobatic dancer in Noo Yoick' before returning to her native land to invest her profits in the present business establishment. High class, she said it was, all her girls had their own rooms. Glorious seven troop, it appeared, had captured one of the innumerable brothels of Athens. One more little honour in keeping with our battle record.

Girls firmly confined in their rooms, troops even more firmly ordered to keep away from them and Bowery Kate organised as cook, we settled into our positions again and surveyed the street before us.

There was little sign of activity, apart from the occasional rifle shot in our general direction, until an accurate burst of machine-gun fire whipped through a window riddling a pile of small packs stacked against the opposite wall for convenience. Incensed at this cavalier treatment of their personal belongings, seven troop worked up their first enthusiasm for the job and set about locating the offending gunner.

We spotted him comfortably established on a small balcony some two hundred yards down the street. Only the muzzle of his weapon projected from a very substantial wall of sandbags. Several bursts of Bren did not disturb him in the least and only provoked another hail of bullets into our kit.

I observed him cautiously with the glasses. There was no hope of hitting him but I noticed that the brackets underpinning his balcony were wooden. For a short while after, he must have thought the British Army were the world's worst shots, as I put magazine after magazine of Bren gun rounds just below his perch. Splinters flew off the wood in all directions and, after about fifteen minutes of traversing slowly backwards and forwards across the brackets, the whole structure subsided into the roadway with a gigantic crash we could hear even at that distance; balcony, sandbags, spandau, gunner and all.

We laughed so much at the shaken and disconcerted gunner picking himself up from the debris that he was away and into a doorway before we could fire at him.

This was our only success apart from the cat. Since the building was flat topped and joined to other similar buildings, we prudently patrolled the roof from time to time, gaining access from an attic doorway. Around midnight, accompanied by Paddy Monahan, I was about to leave this doorway when Paddy heard a stealthy approach along the tiled roof above our heads. We listened to the slithering progress until it was directly above our heads. With deadly efficiency we raised our tommy guns and fired straight up through the roof.

The unscathed cat took off screeching like a banshee, half of seven troop pounded up the stairs to our assistance, the rest of seven troop and the opposing partisans opened up furiously upon each other in panic and Paddy and I thought it best to state that the partisan at whom we had fired was now gone.

Whether the cat ever recovered from the shock is arguable but it took seven troop and the opposition all the rest of that night to settle down again. Paddy and I kept a very low profile.

Before first light, to our unbounded delight, a section of infantry arrived to relieve us. It was not, as we thought, out of pity for our incompetence but because, wonders of wonders, tanks awaited us at Piraeus.

The trucks carrying us to the docks sped in undignified haste since the city was by no means cleared of E.L.A.S. and we arrived jubilantly alongside a row of the most decrepit armoured vehicles we had seen outside of a cannibalisation dump. There were no complaints. Even if the power traverses would not function and the engines belched black smoke, there was armour around us and the guns would fire.

The pace back from Piraeus to Athens was stately and unhindered. Within a week the city was clear of partisans. Seventy-five mm shells fired point-blank into occupied buildings on a delay setting were much more effective than unenthusiastic tank men playing at infantry. The city cleared, we returned with our ancient tanks to Goudhi once again.

For a very brief period we resumed our former placid existence and it was in the course of enjoying this that George Shaw and I once more came under fire.

With a few friends, we had been celebrating at the local taverna and, as we left around midnight, George suggested that we should visit Poppi and Dina whom we had not seen since our triumphant return. Indeed, he insisted, it would be downright boorish not to call upon them after so long an absence. In our state of alcoholic euphoria it occurred to neither of us that the hour might be a little inconvenient, especially in view of the still unsettled situation around the area.

Full of pleasure and retsina, we knocked upon the high gate to the garden. We waited and tried again. When there was still no response George brightly suggested that we should climb over the wall to knock on the house door.

"It would be rude," he said, "to go away." Exchanging words for action, he shinned up with my assistance and immediately became very vocal as his behind encountered the barbed wire that the Karlov family had wisely installed along the top.

His lamentations ceased abruptly as the house door burst open and a shot gun discharged a load of pellets in his direction. With an agonised yell and a great rending sound, George leaped to the ground, leaving the seat of his pants on the wire, and took off at great speed, his bare backside gleaming brightly in the moonlight. I didn't wait to explain to the Karlovs but followed George in haste, taking care to keep well clear of his shining target.

The whistle of shot from the second barrel passed mighty close but none of it lodged in either of us and we reached camp safely, if dishevelled, from our last experience of being under fire on foot.

Bubble Reputation

*C*leared of partisan activity, a process accelerated greatly by the exuberant use of shellfire from our ancient tanks, Athens settled once again into its previous sleazy routine. We were agreeably surprised to find ourselves regarded as rather heroic figures by the largely anti-E.L.A.S., city dwellers. From rough and licentious soldiery, shunned by all respectable citizens of standing, we had suddenly graduated to saviours of their wealth and lifestyle.

This new status was extremely pleasant, coming as it did after the demoralising effect of our bewildered and ineffectual capers around Athens disguised as infantry.

It soothed our wounded egos and gave us a new social image, not to mention the drinks and other hospitable offerings that came our way. The 'Mavro Kapellas', as we came to be called, were now greatly respected for eliminating the partisans and a little feared too on account of the spectacular damage caused by our enthusiastic use of the 75 mm gun against partisan snipers. All in all a very suitable atmosphere in which to soldier.

We spent our days making long leisurely expeditions, at troop strength, into the pleasant countryside. The object of these trips was to show the flag, or rather our tanks, to any partisans or their wavering supporters who remained in rural Attica. Rather like a half-dozen actors marching repeatedly round a stage to give the illusion of an army, we displayed our decrepit tanks far and wide. Often enough this entailed prolonged halts close to tavernas. What better place to be seen by all the village and how convenient for refreshment of the crews.

So effective became this official jaunting that, long before we wished it to happen, there was not a partisan sympathiser left in the entire district and our agreeable forays ceased in the interests of fuel economy. With a consumption of three gallons to two miles this was not unreasonable but there was worse to come in the form of orders from H.Q. to pack and move to Patras where the partisans still defied authority.

The overland route was far too long and rugged for our geriatric Shermans, we had no transporters and the Corinth canal was still blocked by the sunken ship and shattered rail bridge dumped in it during the German withdrawal. Consequently we were routed by sea around the Peloponnesus. Accordingly we embarked on tank landing ships at Piraeus. Disappointingly, they were British ships offering no prospect whatsoever of edible loot to liberate.

Resigned to a profitless and uncomfortable voyage, we quite welcomed the diversion of a large sea mine bobbing about at some thousand yards distance. A burst of machine gun fire from one L.S.T. missed the mine by several yards. To the accompaniment of derisive cheers from the army the matelots on our own vessel joined in. Streams of tracer bullets ricocheted skywards from the steel casing of the mine without touching the sensitive horns and the cheering grew louder. Both guns abruptly ceased to change belts. Before they could resume their fusillade a solitary rifle cracked out from our own L.S.T. rather like an impudent raspberry in an orchestral pause. With an almighty thud a tall pillar of smoke and water shot skywards, the explosion almost drowning the howls of mirth directed at the disconcerted machine gunners.

Grinning partisans stood around everywhere in Patras, festooned like Christmas trees with arms and ammunition belts. They even waited at the docks to laugh at the pitifully inadequate number of troops that a couple of L.S.T.s could bring in. Apparently they had been laughing for days at the company of Gurkhas who had been disembarked and promptly confined strictly to barracks because they took exception to being objects of mirth to scruffy guerrillas and had announced their intentions regarding the latter. This action had prompted the naive partisans to dub the Gurkhas 'Little boys afraid to come out', a name that induced a murderous anticipation of conflict in the fearless little men of Nepal.

Blissfully unaware that the Gurkhas were confined in order to avert a massacre of partisans, the latter were still grinning like Cheshire cats as our L.S.T.s docked. The dramatic change in their expressions, as the bow doors opened and two squadrons of Shermans roared out, had a pantomime quality about it. Well briefed beforehand about the situation, we made the most of it, revving and clattering our thirty-six ton wrecks unnecessarily and occasionally traversing the turrets so that particular groups might have the privilege of gazing straight down the barrels of the 75mms point blank. No doubt they would have been even less happy had they appreciated that our presence there was mainly to scare them away before the Gurkhas could get at them.

Following the issue of a proclamation that any armed or uniformed partisan remaining within thirty miles of Patras at daybreak would be fired upon, we laagered on the barrack square and spent the night with the Gurkhas. All night long, the city resounded to the clatter of hurrying feet and all night long the Gurkhas slept peacefully, fully clad, with their heads resting on their prepared battle kit.

At six o'clock next morning I was gently shaken awake by a smiling little Gurkha.

"Wake up Johnny! Wake up! Time to chase E.L.A.S.! Hurry Johnny!"

Urged on by these eager enthusiasts, we shrugged on our clothes, started up engines and headed away into the hills above

Patras in an effort to add further impetus to the partisans' flight and put a greater distance between them and the Gurkhas.

Due to the soggy nature of the ground we made no more than a few miles before realising that we were in danger of bogging down en masse in the mud. As we turned back the jubilant Gurkhas surged past us at a steady lope and headed inexorably up into the mountains. They continued at this pace till making contact with the more laggard of the partisans, to the great and largely final discomfiture of the latter.

Diverted to clear a warehouse allegedly still in the hands of a party of diehard guerrillas, seven troop clattered into the loading yard and menaced the obviously deserted building until quite sure it was safe to investigate on foot. A great cheer went up as Whitey staggered out of the warehouse carrying a crate of cognac. Before we left, every tank bore its quota of spirits, some of the bottles slotted into the sponson racks that normally held shells, others still in crates lashed to the engine covers. Fortune still smiled upon us.

A modern Hogarth could have done justice to our light-hearted progress back to the Gurkha barracks. Snatches of ribald song rose above the engine noise as sample bottles were passed around the crews, most of whom had perched themselves outside the turrets for greater convenience in social exchanges with everyone they encountered.

Before settling down to a convivial evening of celebration we moved our kit from the ground floor to the one above for the easier accommodation of the Gurkhas should they return during the night. After a memorable few hours of drink and song in good company, well oiled and happily at peace with the world, I retired for the night. At some point later I awoke in urgent need of relief from alcoholic excess and ran straight out of the room at high speed, forgetting in my pressing haste that we had moved our beds aloft. In total darkness I took off horizontally from the top step of the stairs, legs still twinkling in space. I seemed to hang in limbo a moment before crashing down onto the stone stairs beneath me. All desire thumped from me, I lay groaning in sober penitence before crawling painfully back to bed leaving a fair blood spoor in the doleful progress.

We stayed in Patras for several weeks during which time the tanks were laagered on the docks. The guard mounted over them was a very popular duty since there were always pickings to be had around any kind of shipping.

Luck sailed in for us with an American merchant ship which docked very handily alongside the tanks. Before the first day was out, Whitey had sneaked up the gangplank, investigated the galley and relieved the ship of six large Christmas puddings, no doubt stored for the next festive season.

Whilst he was busy with this reprehensible pilfering, his mates were engaged in earnest conversation with members of the ship's crew. They showed immediate interest in the old Turkish sword which served as a poker to the fire that warmed the guard at night. After listening with rapt attention to Paddy's apocryphal account of its capture, the sailors, with much argument, persuaded him to part with it for a fair fistful of dollar bills.

Whilst Paddy finalised this masterpiece of conmanship, the guard commander joined the circle round the fire carrying a captured spandau machine-gun. The Americans' eyes glistened at the sight of such a trophy to display when they returned Stateside and a financially rewarding exchange was speedily agreed upon. At this point, Paddy made his master stroke.

"Howd on!" he said, "Ye've no ammunition for that, boys."

Off he went to the nearest tank and returned with two belts of Browning .300 rounds.

"Hard to come by," he explained, "What's it worth, then?"

Several more dollars changed hands and our customers departed, happily cradling a German machine-gun and belts of American ammunition that would not fit.

Our mirth had hardly subsided when a further deputation arrived from the ship, led by an unfriendly looking type in a white overall. Whitey hastily removed himself from the vicinity as this character began to comment on the thieving bastard who had removed his Christmas puddings. One of our number had apparently been observed going down the gangway. We exuded injured innocence but, unlike his shipmates, the cook had encountered limey soldiers before and was becoming very pointed in his remarks about their lack of integrity when Paddy saved the day with a little touch of genius.

Each day, the fire was crudely but effectively lit by throwing a handful of cordite under the sticks and applying a match. To obtain the cordite, one took a solid shot armour piercing 75 mm round and tapped the shell hard on the front of a tank until it parted from the case. This released the cordite propellant which was sufficient for quite a few fires. The detached solid shot stood upright by the fire, its conical nose stuck into the ground with the flat rear end containing the large magnesium tracer uppermost.

As the argument grew more heated, Paddy surreptitiously placed a red hot ember onto the tracer. Within a couple of seconds the latter ignited with a blinding red light and a fearsome hissing sound.

"Run!" bellowed Paddy, "Run! It's going up!"

We all scattered in great haste for a good ten yards and then stood listening to the rapid footfalls of our visitors disappearing into the far distance. The tracer burnt out harmlessly, the new guard relieved us and we hastened into the city to convert our ill-gotten gains into retsina, ouzo and all the delights dear to the hearts of expatriate soldiery.

Roscoe's End

*O*ur partisan scaring duties concluded at Patras, we moved northwards to Salonika, still in our role of Bogey Men to any remaining E.L.A.S.. Routed overland, to make our presence known as widely as possible, we had our own moments of unease negotiating hairpin bends on the mountain roads.

Thirty-six tons of tracked vehicle skeetering around the abrupt turns, with sheer drops of five hundred or more feet just inches from the offside track did wonders for the organs of elimination. On two occasions we saw eagles wheeling below us, surely a unique sight from a tank turret.

There was nothing remarkable about Salonika except the wonderful carpet of Autumn crocuses in the hills above the city. All was peaceful and there was no need for any histrionic aggression from us. After a stay long enough for the inhabitants to ponder on our dubious might we returned south to Kefissia, a formerly fashionable suburb of Athens.

Here we were luxuriously billeted in a very large hotel, the unexpected shortcomings of which caused grievous discomfort to one of our number.

The whole blame for Roscoe's deplorable injuries could be laid fairly and squarely upon the woeful inadequacies of the Greek drainage system. All of B Squadron had been billeted in the Kefissia Grand Hotel for less than a week before a very pressing problem became pungently apparent. Plumbing that had sufficed as an efficient disposal network for some hundred genteel tourists proved dramatically to be incapable of dealing with the healthy output of thrice that number of hairy-bottomed soldiers. The Squadron Sergeant Major very adequately described the ensuing atmosphere in terms that were explicit but best left unquoted.

A serious stoppage was apparent, and in gunnery parlance, immediate action was required. The issue being urgent, paper piled high. In the office that is. Innumerable forms were completed in triplicate and despatched. Urgent requests for advice and assistance were made to regimental headquarters and duly passed along the line to Brigade Administration. Nothing happened while the buck was being happily passed from one chairbound warrior to another, until the unexpected visit of a senior staff officer. His stay was short, his comments rivalled those of the S.S.M. and abruptly the drama of the situation was pressed to the exalted heights of Corps level.

The ponderous official machinery creaked into motion and in due course the solution to our problem arrived singing lustily. A truck load of Greek navvies, bearing shovels and large containers of retsina, drew up at a spot beside the hotel and overlooking the square.

Operation Ordure proceeded. The workmen began to dig. They dug with uncharacteristic vigour and speed until they slowly disappeared from sight. Shovelfuls of earth flew up from the depths on wings of song and resinous wafts of retsina. A cavernous pit took shape redolent of wine and garlic-laden breath.

Hardened campaigners paused to survey the excavation in wonder. It measured six yards by three, no less, and ten feet deep. The sides were squared to perfection and shored with heavy timber to avoid any premature collapse beneath the straining soldiery. Some wag from H.Q. spread a rumour in the division that ancient gold had already appeared on the black market from the illicit archaeological delving of the forty-third.

At long last the day arrived when the tipsy strains of 'Agappea Mou' no longer floated from the depths. Gathering together their long-handled shovels, cheeses, garlic cloves and wicker bound flagons of retsina, the navvies departed, to be replaced by crafts-men with yet a further truck load of timber.

Speculation grew in pace with the construction. Various esti-mates ranged from eight to twelve, but, on conclusion, everyone eyed with reverence the sixteen smoothly rounded holes that grew in the wooden capping of the depths. Not a single splinter marred the perfection. All was smoothly comforting. Each seat had its own wooden lid securely hinged with leather straps. Our thrones were fly proof and pristine. Sedentary comfort was ensured and still the edifice progressed. Stout wooden walls arose around the seats of meditation. It was no coarse shelter this. The close fitting tongue and grooved boards, the corrugated roof and closing doors all promised sheltered repose. A place to meditate and rest. A veritable valhalla for tavern-weary warriors.

As our new pavilion came into use the malodorous aura sur-rounding the Grand Hotel began to disperse. Personnel from other units no longer avoided our area. We were again socially acceptable, respectable and sanitary members of society as before. Contentment lay upon the squadron. Even the tanks had an air of easeful maintenance about them.

Alas for all the small good things of life. Little by little the lin-gering scents of the navvies' garlic and retsina departed from our palatial latrine and the S.S.M. was again heard to comment coarsely upon the smell replacing them and the perversity of nature which was rapidly returning us all to square one.

Our original miasma returned inexorably with the passing of each day. Depth alone had failed to overcome the odour and dis-infectants were wholly unobtainable.

The sanitary orderly, a reinforcement newly arrived from England, was not overburdened with intelligence but he was keen and eager to show initiative. He had a ready ear for old sweats' tales and he heard that in the Western Desert petrol had been the answer to such pressing problems as now beset him. When the desert roses ponged in the hot African sun a gallon or so sufficed to sweeten them. Armed with a jerrican, he industriously put into practice his newly-acquired knowledge.

The dragon's teeth were sown and Roscoe's card was marked. In the still small hours he lurched from his bed across to the latrine to ease the evening's debauch from his protesting gut. Blissfully seated in peaceful comfort, he lit his cigarette, parted his hairy thighs and threw the match below.

When the general alert had been cancelled, the regiment stood down and the last of the smouldering ruins pushed into the reeking pit, Roscoe departed to hospital, face down upon his stretcher.

His injuries in no way impeded his vocal abilities and the full and detailed account of the personal and very private habits of the sanitary orderly that he gave before his departure was long remembered. Neither did he forget to mention in his blessings the old sweat who had omitted to state that a desert rose was burned out with petrol and not perfumed by its vapour.

When pressed for details on his return to the squadron, Roscoe was heard to state that he had been impressed not so much by the almighty explosive 'whoosh' and roar of flame as by the military machine-gun tattoo of hinged lids flying open.

About his personal injuries he remained very reticent, but it did not escape notice that his evening recreation took him to a different quarter of Athens for some considerable time. Whether this was because of Pavlovian aversion or some physical modification was never disclosed even to his closest friends.

Orchi Despinis!

*P*addy and I were browned off. In the current vernacular we had had it up to the throat. "It's leave we want," I said, "Local leave in Athens."

Paddy outlined a very coarse analogy of our chances in this direction and continued to gaze thoughtfully across the tank park in the direction of the city.

When Paddy became thoughtful like this we knew that he was busy reasoning. He was always very strong on reasons; not logic, just reasons. I waited hopefully for the outcome of his meditations. His thoughts crystallised at length and he turned back to me.

"Guard duty at Christmas time," said Paddy. "We were both on guard duty over all the Christmas period."

"So what?" I said. "We were on rota. It was just our bad luck, that's all."

"Forty-eight hour leave we missed," responded Paddy. "The

142

rest of the squadron had a full two days."

"We had it afterwards," I said. "Remember?"

"But not at Christmas," insisted Paddy. "It was special leave and never recorded. We're still due for leave on the books."

"After two months? You'll be lucky!"

"Give it a go," said Paddy. "We'll request O.C.'s interview."

We did and Paddy won. Not on the logic of his dubious reasoning but the admiration of the squadron commander for his colossal cheek.

Jubilantly waving our leave passes to Athens and leaving an address where we could always be contacted, Yanni's Bar, we departed for the city.

In deference to Paddy's sense of priorities we made for the taverna nearest to where our transport had dropped us in the city centre. After a drink or two, I tentatively ventured to suggest that it might be more prudent to find accommodation for the night whilst still clear headed but the idea was swept away on a flood of Irish eloquence and retsina.

Paddy sat and imbibed the local wine as though it were his native Guinness, scorning glasses and drinking straight from the metal oka measure in which it was brought to the table. He was a very slightly built lad and had an almost feminine regularity of features with the clear complexion that only comes from Ireland.

An innocent in uniform one might think, as many unfortunate mothers of nubile daughters had previously thought. His appearance had always been an 'Open Sesame' to any household in Blighty prepared to tolerate a swaddy's knees beneath the table. Here in Greece his fair skin and guileless expression had disarmed more than a few chaperones of Hellenic virtue. We all knew him for what he was, a Celtic wolfhound in sheep's clothing where the girls were concerned.

He drank steadily at twice my pace and before long my own condition dictated that the time had come to seek rooms for the night whilst still sufficiently coherent. Prising the reluctant girl from his knee and the glass from his hand I ignored his voluble protests and persuaded him out into the street.

Athens was uncommonly full of hostelries and large rooming houses so we anticipated no difficulty in finding a billet. With money in our pockets and a special leave to celebrate, we determined to spend the night in the luxury of a first-rate hotel, perhaps not quite the Britannia but at least some place worthy of our patronage. Our packs could be dropped, we thought, at the first good one we saw.

At this first choice we met with an unexpected blank refusal. It was smoothly disguised by great regrets that all the rooms in the clearly half empty building were occupied but the message came through very clearly. "Rough and boozy soldiers in my beds? Never!"

"Proper appreciation of the heroes of liberation," remarked Paddy. "Should have lobbed a seventy-five round or two in there during the troubles to modify his outlook a bit."

We altered course for a sleazier quarter in the hope of a more understanding reception.

Stumbling up the stairs of the first rooming house to be found, we tackled the proprietor about beds for the night. His smiling acquiescence was immediate and welcoming.

"Why yes, gentlemen. Twenty drachmae for the rooms, forty drachmae the girls."

"No girls," we chorused. "Beds only. *Orchi despinis!* No girls!"

"*Orchi Despinis?*" This in tones of utter disbelief. "All right. I make special price for you. Girls thirty drachmae."

"*Orchi despinis,*" I patiently explained. "We do not want any girls tonight."

"No crumpet!" coarsely put in Paddy. "We shall be fit only for sleep when we come in, matey. Beds, ye bloody heathen! To sleep in!" and he broke into a routine of mime and snores that would have done credit to Marcel Marceau.

"Extra special for you then, Johnny. Girls twenty drachmae!"

"Stuff your girls," yelled Paddy. "Rooms!"

The proprietor gazed apprehensively at the two unnatural beings before him, repudiating his carnal offerings, and fearfully shut the door in our faces, muttering in wonder: "*Orchi despinis. Po! Po! Po! Orchi despinis!*"

We roused the slumbering guardian of the next establishment from his siesta and acquainted him with our needs. His world weary countenance cracked into the semblance of a smile. Here were soldiers on leave with drachmae in their pockets. He yawned vastly and began his routine gambit towards parting us from a little money.

"Rooms very clean. Retsina, ouzo, very cheap."

Paddy beamed at me. In at last! Then came the blow.

"Girls young. Very pretty, very good. Jig-jig all night. Sixty drachmae. That all. No pay any more." His hands carved the air dramatically in explanation of the excellence of his package deal.

Very slowly, very clearly, Paddy expressed our desire to sleep peacefully and entirely unjigged. The incredulous patron regarded us in an outraged manner. "No girls, no beds!" he firmly insisted and followed up with a flood of Greek which paraphrased to "Where's my ruddy profit?"

He resumed his interrupted siesta and the interview was closed.

Responses to our further attempts to find a resting place varied from polite refusal to downright aspersions on our manhood and potency and it was with no great confidence that we approached our final trial.

A wide gold-toothed smile greeted us across the counter. Welcoming wafts of garlic enveloped us along with the now familiar "Beds and girls. Very good. Very clean."

"No girls," ventured Paddy. *"Orchi Despinis."*

"Orchi despinis?" echoed gold tooth in puzzlement, "No girls for bed?"

"No girls" repeated Paddy and again in Greek. *"Orchi Despinis."*

Gold tooth broke into raucous laughter. "Ah! You make the English joke. How is it? You pull me the leg. No girls! That very good. Why you want bed then?" and he gave vent to more appreciative mirth.

Once more we slowly and carefully informed the gentleman that we had no need of girls, all we wanted was a bed for the night.

He gazed speculatively at Paddy for a long moment and then glanced at me. Understanding illuminated his oily countenance.

"No girls? Andaxi! I understand. You not like girls. One room only. One big bed. You, him good friends.'"

He was leering and rubbing his two forefingers together suggestively when Paddy went over the counter at him, with a wild

Irish screech. I caught Paddy by the collar and managed to haul him off before he damaged Gold-tooth and our chances of a bed.

"Be still, you gormless twit!" I shouted. "Pay up. At least we've got a bed for the night!"

The Last Stand

Unwillingly torn from the flesh pots of Athens by the wisdom, or whim, of higher command's decision, we laagered the tanks on the quayside at Corinth and sought out the billets allotted to each troop.

Corinth, at that time, was a small town with none of the tower block hotels and amenities that deface it today. There were several tavernas and a brothel, the latter conveniently and discreetly situated half a mile out of town on the Athens road. Even the old pre-war holiday resort of Loutraki, across the Gulf of Corinth, had only its mineral spa, a large empty hotel and a cluster of streets running parallel to the waterfront.

All this seemed very small beer compared with the night life Athens had offered us, yet we soon found that there was to be never a dull moment in our new small-time urban location.

Since no barracks or large buildings had been built in Corinth, we were billeted troop by troop in the larger houses of the area near to the tanks. Seven troop took over the ground floor of a residence in which the family still lived above.

We shared the garden and the well providing our water with the Greek

147

family and an excessively aggressive nanny goat. The only time the goat showed any amiability was during our ablutions by the well. It had a passion for soapy water and always broke off hostilities to beg for a draught of it. At any other time no-one dared turn his back on the animal and several of us had well-bruised buttocks to testify to the power of its charge. The beast would wander at times into the billet and on one occasion devoured a full set of webbing equipment, a feat that would have been beyond a shredding machine.

It was impossible not to become domesticated in such a situation. There was housework to be done and, next door, lived a mother only too willing to hand her very young baby over the garden wall to be nursed and pampered by the doting foreign soldiery. At times the baby spent whole afternoons happily gurgling in the arms of some hairy-chested hardbitten trooper who cooed and chuckled at it like a besotted maiden aunt. Bill Wilde, in particular, mothered this fortunate scrap, preparing extra feeds with baby food obtained from the Red Cross and volunteering for additional billet duties in order to care for his surrogate offspring.

There was very little work to be done apart from routine tank maintenance and our daily life was pleasant enough, usually ending with a more or less tipsy return home from a favourite taverna each evening. It was after such a return that I fell down the well.

During the horseplay on our way to bed a closed jerrican of diesel fuel had been knocked into the well and, in the cold sober light of dawn, we realised that it must come out before it polluted our drinking water. The well was deep and all our efforts to fish it out with a hook on a long rope were to no avail. Whitey voiced the thoughts of us all.

"Someone will have to go down for it."

As he was the originator of the idea we generously thought that Whitey should have the honour of descent but he would have none of it and quite curtly insisted that we drew lots for the privilege. I drew the short straw.

Feet firmly wedged in the bucket and clasping the rope like grim death, I waited for the three hefties holding the winding handle to lower me below. Slowly I creaked downwards. The parapet passed my vision and I had just begun to admire the delicate ferns growing from the walls when there came a loud crack and multiple yells of anguish from the well top. Simultaneously I dropped like a stone, the windlass above whirring madly as the rope spun from it. Hitting the water at a fair velocity, I floundered around in panic for what seemed an age before realising that if I straightened my legs I could stand upright with my head clear of the water.

I looked hopefully up at the bright disc of light above and strove for enough breath to yell for help. Before I could do so, three anxious faces appeared at the edge.

"Are you O.K. Geoff?" The query echoed lugubriously down the shaft.

When I had answered that I was far from O.K., wet through, cold as charity, bruised and battered but otherwise sound in wind and limb, the heads disappeared again. I stood patiently shivering whilst the howls of uncontrollable mirth resounded down the well.

At length, still stuttering with laughter, the heads reappeared and offered an explanation.

"The bloody handle broke clean off and we all went arse over tip. Damn near ruptured ourselves!"

Whilst expressing deep regret and sympathy for their plight, I asked mildly if they had any immediate plans for my recovery or did they propose to lower food to me on a rope for the duration of our stay in Corinth.

"No need to get stroppy," remarked Whitey, "We'll go and knot together a load of empty browning belts and get enough fellas to heave you out."

In due course I was hoisted out clutching the offending jerrican to my bosom. As I cleared the parapet and stood soggily dripping, the lady of the house appeared. She spoke in some agitation, expressing her opinion of alien idiots who bathed and swam in her drinking water, using terms which threw serious aspersions on my sanity and personal hygiene. I felt too cold to reply.

It was always such sequels of taverna evenings that enlivened our stay in Corinth. A series of incidents, such as the accidental setting alight of so unlikely a vehicle as the filled water truck, culminated in a most memorable battle.

Paradoxically this conflict resulted from the extreme tolerance and sociability of seven troop. Each evening we sought our entertainment in more or less established groups, pooling whatever resources we had when the question of drink or food arose.

Only one of our number patronised the local brothel. This was not a subject for censure or even disapproval by the rest of us but merely an idiosyncrasy like my own addiction to an occasional glass of water with my retsina, a habit regarded as far more unnatural and harmful. Consequently when he felt the urge arise the whole group accompanied him to the brothel, euphemistically known as the casino.

There was no hardship in this. Whilst he was closeted with the lady of his choice the rest of us, for a very modest cost, drank and nibbled various delicacies in the ever amusing company of the temporarily unoccupied work force. Conversation was never dull and on slack evenings, when the girls were relatively unjaded, it ranged from profound discussions to side-splitting anecdotes, delivered with uninhibited turns of phrase that gained added piquancy from the lingua franca in which they were communicated.

This happy situation continued until, one evening, whilst pleasantly waiting for our nameless comrade to conclude his prolonged dalliance, the salon was invaded by a group of Greek civilians who treated our female companions with great disrespect and ourselves with open hostility. They were tolerantly ignored until one of them made reference to Paddy as an English pig.

Paddy patiently explained, before he knocked him down, that the pig was a noble, useful, even Irish creature, and he had no objection to the term, but to be called English to his face was indeed a fighting matter. The Greek concerned lost any further interest in the affair after Paddy had struck him and he lay recumbent throughout the following fracas.

The conflict was heroic. Our hostesses fled screaming and their colleagues deserted the clientele and emerged, some in a state of nature, to find out what was causing the disturbance. They and the abandoned clients took one glance at the mayhem in progress and departed from the scene in great haste, leaving only our amorous comrade who valiantly joined us in battle, clad in nothing but his vest.

Fists, feet, chairs and tables flew in all directions. The room had begun to resemble a wild west film saloon by the time we slung the last of our opponents out of the door.

Immediately after his ejection the real trouble began. One of our late adversaries, almost certainly ex-E.L.A.S., threw a grenade. Fortunately it exploded in the doorway, and being a German 'potato masher' did not fragment too badly. No-one was injured but the noise attracted the attention of a patrol of the Greek Mountain Brigade, already alerted by the previous sound of strife. In full battle order they charged into the wrecked brothel and, without waiting upon the niceties of introduction, we exited over the rear wall of the garden and ran hell for leather towards Corinth and billets, our lusty pal, who had fought berserk throughout, hobbling along with his boots and clothes under one arm.

By morning the affair had been blown up into an armed pitched battle between partisans and an unknown body of tank men. The squadron was duly paraded on the quayside and the brothel patron brought down to identify the culprits. He paused at seven troop, received the concentrated promise of things to come in its concerted glare, and prudently passed on, allowing the incident to quietly slot into the battle honours of the regiment.

Buried in my kit I held a trophy snatched in retreat from this conflict, a large Union Jack which had proudly flown over the brothel alongside the Greek flag.

At a later date I had some difficulty in preserving a sober expression when my mother flew this flag from the house on such occasions as the coronation.

I dared not tell her its origin.

A week or two after the fight I had just started the engines of my tank, as a routine check, when the squadron jeep drew up alongside.

"Hop in!" shouted the driver, "You're going for a medical and C.O.'s interview. Papers have come through. You're being demobbed on 'B' release. Lucky bugger!"

I leaped from the tank as though it were red hot and within

twelve hours I was on my way to board a ship for Italy and the overland route home.

The tank's engines were running when I jumped down from it and for all I know they are running still.

Blanket Cover

*O*verjoyed to see me safely returned from four years' active service overseas, my mother was even more delighted by my newly married status. At long last, she and my father could settle into a tranquil harmony disturbed neither by the presence of a turbulent family nor the wartime anxiety about its safety.

My marriage was a modest and rapid affair, arranged by special licence whilst I was still in transit. Joan was as competent an organiser then as she is today. She often picks me out of the mire into which I sometimes blunder.

The best man was in uniform. I wore civilian clothes since my army gear was very travel-stained and weary. A small child, watching our progress into church, summed up the situation.

"Look Mummy! There's a soldier and an ordinary man going to be married!"

With four blissful weeks of leave before the necessity to work, I began the queer process of rehabilitation to civilian life by learning how to comport myself in a supposedly civilised society. Currency notes had to be carefully slid into a wallet and not stuffed crumpled into a pocket. Adjustment in my approach to civilian folk, who rarely said what they meant and could seldom be relied upon, had to be made. Hardest of all was the concealment of thoughts and opinions, a difficulty that still remains today as a legacy of seven troop camaraderie.

During this period, I made the acquaintance of a future lifelong friend. Harry Greatorex had been recently demobilised to return to his old trade of butchery. His massive good humour and jolly nature carried him through the vicissitudes of food rationing, though not without some mental anguish in the process.

A great eater himself, he could not bear to look at the miniscule cuts of meat that he was forced to weigh and wrap for his customers. Harry had always been a butcher of great sensibility, artistic in the preparation of his meat and genial in his trade. Before rationing he would have suffered a sense of personal failure if a customer had left his shop without the precise cut and quality requested. Now, the jokes and quips he exchanged with his clientele disguised, but never hid, his deep dissatisfaction with the quality and quantity of the meat he had to sell. It distressed him that a customer could no longer take her choice and depart happily laden with a Sunday joint, or chops and steaks unlimited. Rationing, to Harry, became a negation of all his wartime sufferings in the taverns and stews of the Middle East. This was not at all the bright new world of plenty for which he had struggled over his beers in the 'Sweet Melody' in Cairo.

In particular, his rural deliveries caused him great distress. The sight of eminently edible animals made all his out of town deliveries a veritable nightmare. Meat was everywhere. It stood, chewed, bawled and ran in every field. There was meat on the hoof wherever he looked and not a pound of it to be had for his customers.

It is no exaggeration to state that Harry pined. Every mouthful of succulent fillet steak that he ate began to choke him. Customers haunted him by night. In his sleep there were endless queues, crying piteously for aitch-bone and sirloins. Sleepless, he counted imaginary sheep, dangling in mutton cloths in serried rows across his shop window.

Sold right out of his miserable allotment of meat, he scraped and scrubbed his chopping block, re-sharpened his knives and stepped back with a sigh.

A moment later, temptation arrived as Harry stood disconsolately regarding his empty display slab.

"Pig any use to you, mate? Strictly on the 'Q.T.'"

Satan himself stood leaning on his stick, his burly tweed-clad form filling the shop doorway. There was a healthy aroma of manure surrounding him. His ruddy countenance split into a broad grin at Harry's blank stare of disbelief. "It's a good size. You'd have to kill it before you take it away."

Harry wavered for a moment. Perhaps for as long as two moments but certainly no more.

"Where?", he hoarsely whispered, "Where?" Harry had joined the activities of the Black Market.

Tools of the trade carefully concealed, Expedition Pig began at dusk. Harry, assistant and plain van departed farmwards, lusting after meat. They drove carefully as they followed Satan's directions. This was no time to be stopped for speeding or other trivial offence. All must be quiet and unobtrusive until the pig hung in the refrigerator.

Swinging into the farmyard, they stopped, cut the engine and sidled, knives in hand, with true assassins' stealth, into the shadows of the farmhouse porch. Satan greeted them softly and led them to the unfortunate animal.

"Look at that!" whispered Harry, regarding the broad back. Whistling softly, he reached for his knife.

The dark deed perpetrated, the pallid corpse gutted and all the evidence safely buried, the conspirators shook guilty hands in pledge of secrecy before hoisting their victim into the van. Its springs groaned as they laid the massive carcass full length upon the floor.

Harry covered the body with a blanket, tenderly tucking it around to conceal the crime from prying eyes. They had driven out into the lane when Harry abruptly halted the van.

"Nip back and pay," said Harry. "In the panic loading up, we forgot to settle up straight away. We don't want to come near here again unless it's for another pig."

He handed over the blood money to his assistant and lapsed into pleasant reveries of chops and loins and belly pork.

Cycle brakes squealed and a light in the eyes rudely awakened him. A policeman leaned his helmet and caped shoulders into the cab, demanding the purpose of such nocturnal loitering. Harry's honest face shone benignly as he handed over his licence and documents, explaining how a love of nature led him to be parked in a dark country lane at night.

The constable beamed his torch into the rear of the van, illuminating the recumbent blanket-wrapped form reposing there. He switched off the light and turned to Harry.

"And what's this then, lying in the back?"

"Ah!" responded Harry, winking broadly and nudging with the elbow, "And what do YOU think I'd have tucked up under blankets in a dark country lane at this time of night? I only just made it back to the cab when I saw you coming. My pants are still in a twist!"

They guffawed in unison.

"Like that, is it?" queried the constable enviously. "Well I'm no spoilsport." He turned to address the blanket covered pig, "It's all right, lass. I've seen nowt!"

Harry watched him straddle his bicycle and heaved a sigh of relief.

"Choose a better place for your bit of leg-over next time," the constable advised as he pushed down on the pedal.

Learn and Live

*I*n the manner of all life's more enjoyable periods, demobilisation leave raced away at an unseemly speed leaving the dual problems of setting up house and entering the so-called profession of instructing the young. Both proved to be difficult and at times ludicrous.

Utility furniture, often more aptly known as 'futility' in view of its slap-happy manufacture and lack of durability, could only be bought on the production of 'dockets', a type of rationing coupons issued to the newly wed.

Quantity and quality of futility furniture were both wholly inadequate for normal usage and we sat on sadistically uncomfortable chairs with coconut matting covering the floor beneath us. Young love, of course, made light of such trivialities but not of a bed that collapsed beneath us at a crucial intimate moment. We lay in the ruins bruised and hysterical with mirth, a condition not at all conducive to further efforts for quite a while.

Adjustment to my first teaching post proved even harder than the re-arousal of passion after our traumatic descent. Qualified immediately before joining the army, I had never faced a class in anger, or in any other emotion either, and the prospect of so doing filled me with greater dread than the whole of the Hermann Goering Division had ever done.

This dread of the unknown led me during the last few days of leave to attend a teachers' refresher course at Scarborough. Like all such courses it benefited only those who conducted it and disastrously underlined the gulf between my Eighth Army outlook on life and that of my new colleagues.

A chance conversation with one of these teachers on the last day of the course brought home my need for rehabilitation to enter the educational system.

On learning casually that I had recently returned from Greece, he spoke with horror in his voice of an account given to him by a soldier who had been sent to that country for a couple of months following the quelling of the insurrection. This hero had been stationed at Loutraki and told of a tank regiment across the gulf that had been so long overseas that its men were no longer wholly sane and behaved like wild beasts. Apparently they had fought pitched battles in Corinth, even in brothels of all places, and were constantly drunk and violent. I shook my head disapprovingly, tut-tutted and said nothing.

The time came to enter school and, as I had anticipated, soldiering with the Eighth and teaching had little in common. After a wartime of the former, adaptation to the latter proved at first to be well-nigh impossible. The pitiful fragments remaining of teacher training, never very practical at best, were buried deep beneath more basic approaches quite unsuitable to the classroom. Even amongst colleagues, the robust subjects of conversation, normal to a tank crew, dropped into the earnest atmosphere of the staffroom like brick ends down a sewer.

Hardened and cynical I may have seemed to my peers: but, in the classroom, matters were very much reversed. There I was a lamb thrown to the wolves. The stress of facing a class of eager faces, eager for the kill that is, led me at times to lapse into phrases not entirely scholarly. Not that this was even noticed by the pack.

Horror in hearing myself say, "That's arse about face, lad!" was quickly superseded by surprise at the pupil's casual reversal of the sum in question.

Certainly this was lesson number one for me. Say anything earnestly and with great conviction and the content and phrasing will never be questioned. The more astute teachers rocket to the top on this precept without benefit of great ability or intelligence. A simple man myself, I only ever used it in the classroom jungle, which was but a microcosm of the system.

Maintenance of good order and discipline was a nightmare. Hampered by vague recollections of college lectures outlining the supposed evils of corporal punishment, I stood no chance at all. The ruthless, untiring mob eagerly waited to pounce on any weakness shown by the innocent newcomer.

The unlikely intervention of Billy Slater's big feet brought about my ultimate salvation. He sat, or rather slouched, behind Freddie Grant, the scourge of the whole staff. Billy lounged in his normal insolent posture, feet asprawl in the space between desks. Freddie fiddled about, giggling inanely as I paced distractedly between the rows wondering what I should do about him. One step more and I tripped over Billy's feet. Down he slid to the floor whilst I fell heavily upon the neck of Freddie Grant. His face bounced against the desk lid with a heart-warming crunch. Only I remained upright astride the recumbent Billy Slater.

The awestricken class blenched at the howls of anguish and the blood dripping from Freddie's nose. An instantly established reputation for ferocious retribution swept away all problems of discipline.

Still basking in a new found confidence, I thoughtlessly allowed the rabble to hand me the bat during cricket practice, an error likely to bring no good to a born cricketing rabbit. The ball hurtled down. I gave a blind swipe and opened my eyes to a great cheer as the ball soared over the school and out into the street. Modestly laying down the bat I stepped away from the wicket. I never touched a bat again. Thus are reputations made.

The final guarantee of some degree of respect and acceptance came also by accident. Christmas approached and the festive spirit prompted the staff to perform a humorous play as part of the concert.

One of the least sought after parts was that of a character rejoicing in the name of 'Mr Stick-it-up', the brain child, I felt, of a singularly unimaginative playwright. This unfortunate creature, clad in shorts, beribboned, and carrying a galvanised bucket and brush, was to prance around the stage making a general fool of himself. It was inevitable, I suppose, that the role should be thrust upon the most junior member of staff.

Our rehearsals did much to undermine my newly acquired authority. Tittering pupils eyed the ribbons with glee and I came near to receiving the first ever visual nickname. The gesture was certainly expressive.

Pupils and parents assembled expectantly on the sacrificial day. We opened well. Old Skinner, as cook, had taken the wise precaution of placing the script on his pastry board. His energetic rolling caused a certain disorganisation as the script curled round the pin but we ad-libbed valiantly. It was this vigorous impromptu work that took Mr Stick-it-up to the rear of the improvised stage where a dramatic gesture and a step backwards precipitated him through the back-cloth to a drop of several feet.

The clang of the metal bucket across Stick-it-up's bare shins and his anguished calls upon the Almighty, the Educational System and all concerned with the production brought down the house. There were tumultuous roars of appreciation and no-one could doubt the approval of familiar phrases by the recently demobbed fathers coerced into attending the affair. The pupils rolled about in their seats.

As I crawled painfully back from under the hangings, the standing ovation told me that I was there at last! By accident as it were!

The Old School

*M*urphy's old eyes would twinkle merrily when my frequent conversational *faux pas* tore holes of silent disapproval in the staff room discourses. I liked him for that and also held him in great respect for his ability to see the wood instead of a tree or two. He was near retirement and had seen it all including, I later learned, the Gallipoli fiasco of his war.

Most experienced teachers sufficiently intelligent to see beyond the current gimmickry of their job become disillusioned and sour with age. They grow lined, haggard and earnestly conscientious in the performance of scholarly rituals in which they no longer believe.

This was certainly not so in the case of Old Murphy. None came more cynical than he, and none so cheerful.

"My boy," he said. "I long since gave up chasing educational bandwagons. It's a laugh a minute to watch them rattle by with the eager beavers leaping on and falling off again. Some make it,

but most end here with me. At least my knees are unpolished."
His philosophy was as rich as his brogue. "At any given moment
my methods are old fashioned, contemporary or advanced," he
went on. "I don't ever change. The fly boys never realise there's
nothing new in this job. It all comes round for the second or third
time. Stand still, lad, and let it all catch up with you."

God bless Old Murphy. His sound advice saved me a career of
futile activity pursuing the current myths of the system.

He was a betting man, one of the few I ever knew who won at
least as much as he lost, and he scandalised one of His Majesty's
Inspectors by the extension of his sporting instincts to the classroom. This poor man narrowly escaped transfixion by a dart
when he entered Old Murphy's room without knocking. It had
been thrown by an eager pupil at a list of mental sums on the
blackboard. If his luck was good he hit an easy one, if not he
learned the philosophy of acceptance.

Murphy listened courteously to the inspector's remonstrations
and then earnestly explained that this was part of the new incentive concept, the sporting approach to pupils with motivation
problems. Surely the inspector did not expect him to ignore the
current national trend in teaching methods. Unsure of his ground
the H.M.I. uneasily withdrew from the argument.

Occasionally if a persistent offender needed to be caned, Old
Murphy would produce a penny.

"Double or Quits?" he would shout ferociously and if the quak-
ing victim agreed the coin was tossed. Many years passed before
any of us realised that it was always quits and Murphy always
called the side. The penny was double-headed and the sporting
victim always escaped scot-free, blessing his luck, proud of his
gamble and determined not to push his luck with the same
offence again.

The old chap had his own ways of punishment. He was bitten
once whilst breaking up a savage playground brawl. The following morning, a stricken class watched him drag his feet into the
room. He was ebullient no longer and tenderly nursed his heavily bandaged hand. There was no opening bellow and no threats,
only a quiet disturbing Murphy. His class was worried.

Ginger Smedley plucked up courage to ask him how he fared.

"Badly, boy, badly!" he replied and sat down wearily at his desk. Indeed, the hand was bandaged to twice the normal size and he winced at every move. A very uneasy peace lay on the class and when, on the third day, Old Murphy sported a sling and wore a woebegone expression, anxiety grew to near hysteria. The unfortunate who had bitten him now had a black eye, the token of his mates' disapproval. Rumours of blood poisoning and worse were rife and depression lay heavily upon the class at the prospect of a quiet kind-spoken, colourless Murphy.

This dismal situation lasted for the best part of a week before a howl of pure joy resounded from his room. In a forgetful moment he had slipped the sling from his arm and heartily tanned young Jones with the wounded hand. Hoax over, the teeth marks were examined by everyone, Murphy bellowed with mirth and all was well once more.

He retired shortly afterwards, distinguishing himself in the last week during a verbal exchange with an unjustly aggrieved parent. She ear-bashed him fortissimo and threatened a visit to the Education Office. Old Murphy remained poker faced and silent to the end of her harangue. Slowly he drew threepence from his pocket, dropped the coins into the astonished lady's hand and quietly remarked, "Your bus fare, Madam."

Leaving two bottles of Teachers Whisky on the staff room table, he quietly disappeared to his native Ireland.

Nature in the Raw

An academic myth of long standing is the supposed educational benefit to be derived by pupils from trips to various places of questionable interest to them. I suspect that this journeying originated in the desire of ever indigent teachers to tour their own centres of interest at no cost to themselves. This, of course, was extremely short-sighted. The cost in nervous energy expended, physical discomfort and constant anxiety is exorbitant.

Their pupils do benefit, rarely educationally, but in the joy of escape from school, glee at the great difficulty of any maintenance of authority over them once at large and the pleasure of embarrassing members of staff, before a horrified public, in more ways than one can possibly foresee.

However, the custom had long been established before my entry into the maelstrom and it was inevitable that, as a young and still vigorous newcomer, I should organise 'The Trip'.

"You're asking for trouble", I was bluntly told on proposing to take 4C for a coach trip around the beauty spots of the county. The advice came from a senior colleague of long experience. He continued, "You wouldn't remember when Whitley took them to the zoo. He'd lost half of them within an hour. D'you know where he found them? Some chasing the wolves around inside their enclosure and the rest in the middle of the snake pit. Terrified the poor animals. The keeper was most offensive to poor Whitley and requested him never to return in terms Whitley said he wouldn't even have used to 4C."

"It's true," broke in another Chalky type character. "I wouldn't take that lot as far as the next street without slave yokes and a horse whip."

Young and brash, I discounted the sufferings of my predecessor, ignored the sound advice of experienced seniors and continued to organise the trip.

This was a thankless task, the only reaction from 4C being a series of snide remarks regarding the mythical profits I was supposed to be making from the excursion as I collected their money by instalments.

Last contributions prised from them, I ordered the coach. It duly arrived on the appointed day greeted by savage howls of delighted anticipation from my charges. The driver was neither cordial nor enthusiastic when he saw them.

"The company's insurance doesn't cover war and pestilence," he remarked, casting a baleful eye on the seething mob I held at bay.

He watched, poker-faced, as I began to sort them out, confiscating mouth organs, catapults and all other offensive weapons in the process. Eventually, after much pleading and many threats of physical violence, I had them all seated in the coach and clamouring for the driver to take us away.

"You've missed your vocation," he said to me, "You'd have made a good lion tamer. Better paid and safer than this job, too." He threw in his clutch and we were away.

I sat complacently. All were present if far from correct. We rolled along out of the town in comparative peace and order, broken only by the muffled retching of Tosher Tansley into his paper travelling bag. I watched the green fields sliding past my window and relaxed. 4C were not so bad after all in spite of the veterans' warnings. They only needed a bit of firm youthful understanding.

A fierce application of brakes shot me from my seat and shattered my reverie.

The driver, white-faced, leaped to the door.

"We've lost one of the sods!" he shouted. "The rear emergency door indicator just lit up. Somebody's fallen out.'"

Hearts pounding, we raced round to the back of the coach just in time to see the door being stealthily closed. There was no mangled corpse lying in the road, only Ryalls wanting his own private rear view of the countryside.

"If you don't belt him, I will," threatened the driver. Punishment administered and Ryalls transferred to the front of the coach, we continued.

We halted later to commune with nature and I was given much unsolicited and conflicting advice. The toilet attendant and his clients suggested I employ a large cane. Outside, a dear old lady berated me for the frankness of my speech and the laying on of hands in organising the queue. I pleased no-one except 4C who, resenting outside interference of any sort, requested the old lady to go away and mind her own business in terms which modified her outlook on the way in which certain pupils should be addressed.

We reached our main objective at midday, a most beautiful wide trout stream tumbling between mountain slopes. Having lurched across the stepping stones, suffering only one immersion and the loss of two packed lunches, I felt sufficiently euphoric to make a fundamental error of inexperience.

"You can separate now, if you like," I said, "but if you hear my whistle come straight back here."

Before I'd got the sentence out not a boy remained. All had gone, like homing pigeons, straight up the mountainside and onto the scree. The driver gaped at me in horror.

"You've bought it now, mate," he managed to say, and as I grabbed for my whistle we saw Murdoch fall from the rock overhang. He dropped some forty feet, arms and legs flailing wildly.

Panic stricken, I was halfway up the slope before he hit the scree, rolled down like a rag doll and lay ominously still. I picked him up, blood trickling from his head onto my white anorak, and staggered with him down to the riverside. Whilst I straightened him out on the grass the driver ran off along the bank to find a telephone.

Murdoch did not stir and by the time the ambulance arrived carrying the exhausted driver, 4C was almost as anxious as I was. Their solicitous comments had not been calculated to reassure us.

"Is he dead, sir?"

"Has he bust his skull?"

"Look how white he is!"

"Is he still breathing?"

The ambulance men carefully examined him but remained noncommittal.

"His pulse is strong but you can't tell with head injuries."

Murdoch stirred faintly as they lifted him into the ambulance.

"Call at the hospital on the way back and see how he is," they suggested.

Shock and a certain rough concern for Murdoch's welfare caused 4C to behave almost like human beings for the remaining two hours, which was just as well, for I was preoccupied with forebodings. In *loco parentis*, I had failed miserably.

My first trip likely to end with a maimed and possibly dying boy, I could see my career ending almost before it began.

On the way back to school we drew up at the hospital.

"You stay and look after this lot," said the driver, "I'll go and see how he is."

I don't think he fancied being left on his own with 4C. I was sitting, gathering strength to hear the bad news, when a jaunty figure swung onto the coach, a bloodstained bandage round his head.

"Where's me grub? I could eat a scabby monkey! Gave me nowt to eat in there!" Murdoch, the delicate, was once more amongst us.

The remarks of my colleagues on my wild-eyed, bloodstained return were expected but the driver's parting shot rankled.

"Let me know when you plan another trip," he said, "I'll have a day off".

Comrade

There are those teachers who find real satisfaction and genuine excitement in the instruction of their charges. The tiny incidents of each day evoke a sense of eventfulness in their lives and, dare I say it, a whisper of power in the microcosm of school life. I have never ceased to envy these souls. True, I could always laugh at the antics of the establishment, the pitfalls into which I regularly fell, the classroom humour and the schoolboy howlers, but any stronger emotion escaped me. Endless repetition and sameness of constantly rehashed methods form a very close horizon.

This attitude and a very happy home life proved a great drawback to advancement in the profession. Courses, meetings, seminars, rubbing up against all the right folks, fell by the wayside when competing with domestic comforts. I was always a home loving type and therefore it was with mixed feelings that I learned that I was to become a father.

Apart from doubts about the desirability of propagating my own individual characteristics, delight at the prospect of parenthood was mixed with some apprehension at the thought of future interruptions of the even tenor of our household harmony.

In all fairness I must state that my wife was most considerate and nursed me diligently through her pregnancy with none of the foibles or sicknesses frequently associated with her condition. The crunch only came when her time was due.

I have always found that the weaker sex is a feeble specimen when deserted by its women. Left in grave anxiety by their inconsiderate wives for such trifles as confinement, the poor male suffers inordinately. Not that Joan was at all thoughtless when she departed early one morning for the maternity ward of the local hospital. Before ringing for the taxi she wrote out my standing kitchen orders, posted them upon the pantry door and made me a cup of tea to steady my nerves.

This was splendid but none of it prevented her departure. Ten minutes later and I was left alone, chewing my finger nails in apprehension. Pulling myself together with an heroic effort, I marshalled my utensils for the week, a plate, a mug, knife, fork and spoon. The standing orders took care of provender and menu. My morale rose as I read the list. Organisation had triumphed. There was nothing to it!

Alas for over-confidence. As the empty tins piled higher on the drainer I was forced to raise my culinary ambitions. I was not too worried. After all, the very best of chefs are always male.

I started in a humble way. Rice pudding is hardly one of the world's exotic dishes. A pint of milk, a pound of rice, well stirred and set inside a hot oven, presented no great problem.

It was about an hour before the rice appeared around the bottom of the oven door. Like Vesuvius in eruption, it oozed down to the floor. Acrid smoke drifted from the door edges. Cautiously I opened the oven. It was full of pudding. The dish had completely vanished beneath the swollen product of its contents. Mournful but undaunted, I scraped the oven approximately clean. A brief study of the cookery book cast light upon my quantitative errors but I lacked the courage to make a second attempt.

Rock cakes, I argued, must be very simple. Even the wartime

NAAFI had supplied them and if they could produce an edible comestible then it must be a very fundamental confection. After studying the recipe with care, I kneaded the mixture, placed my offerings on the oven shelf and timed them carefully.

At least my rock cakes stayed docilely within the oven. It took some effort, I must add, to prise them out. Their durability was remarkable. I failed miserably to mark them with my teeth and threw them out for the birds. Wind and rain failed to crumble them. My son was three months old before a heavy frost disintegrated them upon the rockery.

While I was still cleaning the mixing bowl my wife's friend Jane paid me a visit. Glad of a sympathetic ear in which to pour my troubles, I did not listen too closely and her talk of christenings, cakes and sherry made little impact on me. Not until she had gone did I think of her kindness to be baking me a cake.

The cake arrived and the size and richness of it astounded me. With almond paste and icing upon it there would have been a Christmas cake before my grateful eyes. It was as delicious as it looked. Enough remained after four days to take a huge slab to my wife during visiting hours.

At the sight of it she recoiled onto her pillow in horror.

"That's the Christening Cake!" she gasped. "Jane said she would bake it. You've eaten up the Christening Cake!"

Recovering from the shock rather faster than I did, she spelt out a scheme to avert disaster.

"Go straight round to Mother," she said. "Tell her what's happened."

I did.

Calculation of the original size from the remaining sector and detailed analysis of the ingredients by mother-in-law enabled her to bake a duplicate.

The cake was duly cut after the christening and, without comment, almost too expressionless, Jane ate her portion.

Many years have passed since then and still I cannot meet her eye. Did she know? I wonder.

Sam

There are few compensations to offset the dreary routine of a teacher's day, but, just occasionally, a pupil of note does wonders for morale. He is seldom the conscientious academic type, usually quite the reverse. Sam was just such a lad. No boredom could exist when he was around. There was plenty of exasperation and provocation but never a dull moment for his teacher.

Nowadays he would have been classed as a member of that section of society known as the underprivileged. Sam would have vigorously repudiated such a description being well aware of all the opportunities, skills and worldly wisdom he enjoyed to a degree unknown to his more pampered class mates, for whom he felt both scorn and sympathy.

Above all Sam was a champion of the underdog. In school he was my implacable enemy. Once outside the building we were the best of friends. Within the confines of the classroom I stood as a symbol of tyranny, an object to be challenged. On the street, in authority no longer, I belonged to Sam's own category of the underprivileged, a teacher, barred by the nature of his job from all the robust pursuits of his own parent. To Sam I was a financial and cultural pauper very worthy of his consideration.

New members of staff found his attitude very disconcerting. In the morning he might roundly abuse his form master for punishing a mate of his, only to sidle up later in the day and offer his Dad's services to thump another aggressive parent. He was not one of nature's intellectuals but he was full of compassion for those down on their luck or, like himself, oppressed by authority. Friend or foe according to circumstance, Sam remained the infinitely variable factor to ensure that no teacher ever became complacent.

I was entering school one dinner-time, carrying a battered, rusty tricycle when Sam accosted me.

"Wot yer got that fer?" he demanded.

Explaining that I could not afford to buy a new one, I told him of my plans to renovate and paint it for my infant son's birthday.

"Yer got it off 'im, didn't yer?" Sam pointed down the road to the receding rag and bone horse and cart. "Owmuch?"

Diffidently I admitted to the expenditure of five shillings. Sam recoiled. His horror was dramatic.

"Yer've bin done. Why didn't yer tell me? I could ah got it fer a tanner!" Only a hasty grab at his collar prevented him from dashing off to recover the squandered four and sixpence from the oppressor of the innocent.

Following this incident, Sam decided that I was too vulnerable and gullible to be any threat to him, in or out of the classroom, and threw a protective shield about me. A minion of authority I might be, but very much in need of care and protection in his eyes. Sam considered me from then onwards as not fit for the jungle outside school, an innocent abroad in need of guidance.

His presence in class imposed a certain restraint upon the teacher's initiative. Any request to bring in useful odds and ends for class use was fraught with danger if Sam was there. He had a tendency to arrive the following day, laden with all that was necessary and followed only too often by a visit from the local 'bobby'.

Such an embarrassment followed my rash appeal for gravel to refurbish our class room aquarium. Sam staggered in the next day, bearing two buckets full of beautiful green marble chippings.

These had hardly been admired and installed in the fish tank before the policeman arrived in the classroom. Some juvenile miscreant, it seemed, had disturbed the surfaces of several graves in the nearby cemetery and chalked rude words on the path with the beak of a marble dove. It was suspected that he was from this school. His mate's eyes swivelled to Sam and on to the aquarium but no-one shopped him.

My last encounter with Sam was shortly after he had left the school. He was standing on the pavement beneath a G.P.O. linesman who was working at the top of a telegraph pole. Another linesman came along and took the ladder to ascend the next pole. Sam turned to me in great indignation.

"They've taken that poor bugger's ladder away!"

I hastily fled before our champion of the underdog swung into action.

In All Sizes

$\mathcal{S}$ choolboys come in all categories, excellent, good, indifferent and bad. It is perhaps because teachers become hardened to the last type that occasionally they suffer from the other extreme. Not that they wish for a lack of eagerness and ability. The first quality is rare and the latter priceless, but one can have too much of a good thing and certainly it was a bright boy who drove me, in desperation, to request a lower stream for two years in succession before regaining courage to risk another Horsley.

Arriving from another school, untainted by our humanly fallible approach, he sparkled with eagerness. Spotless, tidy, radiating alertness, he entered his new school and class ahead of the others. Ignoring the noisily shambling multitude behind him he headed straight for my desk and courteously extended his hand.

"My name is Horsley. I'm the new boy from London. I am sure we shall have a good year together, Sir."

I muttered a reply, indicated a vacant desk and he sat down

smoothly, leaving me with a vague sense of inferiority. His introductory assumption of a pleasant twelve months of mutual association was to have been my opening gambit. My own welcome to the class had been snatched away.

"Get on with these!" I snapped and scribbled hastily upon the blackboard to hide my discomfiture.

Horsley's work was unfailingly faultless. I hated to mark it. By contrast, any written comment of mine looked like the illiterate scrawl of the sub-normal. He looked after me. Indeed, he looked after everyone whether they desired it or not. The class was never unprepared, and improvisation became a thing of the past. Everything was always ready for the opening of each lesson. Horsley saw to that. Gradually he began to extend his helpfulness to the progress of the curriculum.. To begin with he just occasionally interrupted the lesson being taken to improve some aspect that he considered inadequately covered or lacking in precision.

"Excuse me, Sir," he would say with impeccable politeness, "Wouldn't it seem more explicit if we expressed it this way?"

And, of course, he was always right, completely destroying my lesson with the best of intentions.

He soon began to suggest the course of the lessons and later the subject matter itself. Left to himself I am sure he could have very adequately replaced me. Unfailingly courteous, at the end of a period he would usually congratulate the teacher concerned if he thought a reasonable lesson had been given, remarking that he had very much enjoyed such and such an aspect of it.

On one occasion when the head was out of school for a week and the secretary ill, we installed Horsley in the administrative office to report any telephone calls. It was also a golden opportunity to get him out of my hair for a while. There were never any messages from him and it was some time before we realised that Horsley was conducting the whole of the school business himself, answering all queries from parents or the local authority. We found later that he had verbally agreed to the purchase of several batches of essential school supplies suggested by educational firms and was personally responsible for the acceleration of many long overdue items.

It was, paradoxically this assumption of complete authority that brought about his downfall. Having carefully noted a message from the Education Office, he sent round a courteous efficient warning that one of Her Majesty's Inspectors of Schools was to visit us the next day.

Great was the panic and preparation. By afternoon all was ship-shape. At the appointed hour, the following morning, the school nurse walked in.

"Ready for head inspection?" she asked.

Horsley never recovered from his interpretation of Head Inspector as H.M.I.

His grip was loosened and the school relaxed into normality.

No doubt, in due course, Horsley passed into administration somewhere. I wonder which branch he graces?

Not quite contemporary with this paragon of virtue were two other pupils worthy of especial mention. They were both of an age to be in my class. One was that universally despised creature, the school bully, big for his age, timorous of even larger boys and merciless towards any smaller or inoffensive lad who showed any fear. A potential victim of this character, a small frail-looking boy rejoicing in the name of André, proved to be a much more notable character.

The school lived in terror of Billy Summerton, the bully. His size and nature brought misery and tears to many a little lad. Unlike most of his kind, he was moderately intelligent. This made detection very difficult to achieve. He chose his moments, intimidated witnesses and his victims were always too afraid to bring complaints to the staff.

This was the situation when André Staveley, an undersized, pale boy arrived in the form. There was an almost ethereal quality about his apparent fragility. He said very little and worked steadily. Nothing about him indicated that Summerton's days of bullying were numbered.

In retrospect, the staff should have noticed one or two oddities about the weakly André. He was hopeless at games, an absolute rabbit on the field, and yet no-one taunted him about it. In the jungle life of school, this in itself was remarkable. At breaktime, he would walk quietly in the playground and the howling mob around never seemed to barge him. If he chose to sit and read, no scorn was poured upon him.

The first indication of his hidden potential occurred during a science lesson. Each group worked with a magnet and two dozen inch iron nails. After a few minutes, André's partner wandered out complaining.

"Sir," he announced, "we've no nails left",

In response to the resultant query, he explained, "I bet André a bob he couldn't swallow a nail and he's scoffed his four and mine as well!"

This information caused me above a little consternation and we flew to panic stations immediately. Whilst we flapped around him, the unperturbed André ate his cotton wool sandwiches with the same aplomb that he had shown whilst swallowing the nails.

A phone call to his parents elicited a calm response.

"Don't worry," his mother said. "He'll be all right if that's all he's done." He was,too, which is more than could be said for me. By lunch time I was strained in mind and vision through anxious scrutiny of the undismayed André.

In the afternoon of the same day, Billy Summerton did not appear at registration time. He finally arrived in the custody of the Deputy Head.

"Look at this.'" said the latter. "Deserved every bit of it, I expect, but we'll have to go through the motions of investigating things."

A tram accident could not have bettered the injuries to the bully's face. Cuts, abrasions, tear streaks covered it. He limped and sagged and blubbered louder than any of his victims ever had.

"Who knows anything about this?" demanded the Deputy, concealing his delight with great difficulty. André stood up immediately. His explanation was Biblical in style. "I laid my hands on him," he said, "I laid my hands on him and he fell down."

When the roar of mirth had subsided, this modern miracle was more fully explained. The hands had been laid upon the chest of the bully and a sharp thrust had sent him base over apex onto André's pal conveniently kneeling behind his legs. When Summerton's head had bounced off the kerb the frail and ethereal André had jumped repeatedly upon him with both feet before bashing his face several times on the road surface.

Billy Summerton, prestige and legend gone, never struck again.

A la Môde

*P*rogress in education is rather like the changing fashions of ladies' clothing. Styles change continuously and to be 'with it' one must never be seen to be wearing the wrong suit of methods. Dress hemlines go up and down; likewise the do's and don'ts of the educational merry-go-round.

Endless successions of courses take care of this, rolling out bandwagons for the ambitious to leap upon. They constantly alter the superficialities of method, often completely reversing the policies of previous educational dogma. Every now and then the super-course appears. This is when someone on high has a name to make or a financial axe to grind. Always it is the method to end all methods. Till the next one comes around. New maths, new science, instant advanced learning for all. No matter that few are qualified to teach the new subject matter. Enthusiasm is all. The blind lead the blind in earnest expertise, to the vast amusement of the few knowledgeable ones who remain invariably sceptical.

Such a course did I attend some years ago, a course to transform our dimmest pupils to potential scientists. We listened in wonder to the eulogy of marvellous new methods to convert our sows' ears into technical silk purses. The evils of our previous ways were laid down before us with the fervour of a hell-fire preacher of the eighties. Furthermore, the fiat had gone forth. We must all practise what was preached.

We did. A simulated class, composed of teachers, was assembled and the apparatus of this wonderful new horizon laid before us. Bricks were weighed, batteries connected, beads counted, pendulums swung, conclusions reached. What about, no-one seemed to know, but doubtless it was all important, there was such activity. This we found was the key word. Activity! So long as there was activity, no matter how chaotic or futile, all was well. The children were discovering!

My own efforts to push a stick through a swinging blob of plasticine being somewhat abortive, I made notes of my conclusions as requested. From their reception by the earnest drivers of the bandwagon, I do not think that my comments on the experiment were quite what was required. Retiring hurt, I applied myself to observation of the deeds of the enlightened.

A mature gentleman was experiencing considerable success in making pennies fall to the bottom of a glass of water. He was equally good at floating corks on top. His conclusions were exemplary.

"I have discovered," he announced dramatically, "that copper sinks and cork floats." It seemed a pity that the effect was marred by his sly wink and muttered "Eureka!" A heretic, I thought, and hastily drew aside.

Two young Deputy Heads of more sincere demeanour drew small weights up inclined ramps. One ramp was polished smooth, the other surfaced with sandpaper. Their somewhat startling conclusion that it was easier to pull the weight up the rough slope because friction prevented the weight from slipping backwards, lost all chance of promotion for a young and junior teacher.

"What?" said the tactless one. "You drive up hill with your brakes on to make your car go faster?"

Needless to say, with such lack of original thought, the young man still remains at the bottom of the ladder.

Fired with make-believe enthusiasm, I returned to school to act out the charade. My classroom was soon a model of advanced approach. Strings, beads, boxes, batteries, weights and bricks lay everywhere. Eager pupils milled around investigating them and occasionally testing the durability of one another's heads.

It was a great shame that the Head, noted throughout town for his excellent results, was so unappreciative.

"Get this rubbish out of here," he said. "We still work in this school."

In The Heights

In the fullness of time I was appointed to the exalted heights of Deputy Headmaster. This did not unduly puff me up with pride since the post is that of general dogsbody, despite its high-sounding title, and carries a status level slightly below that of an efficient school caretaker who at least performs a visibly useful function.

Even the circumstances of my appointment were somewhat ignominious. The Head of the school wanted me as his Deputy but a gentleman with very real influence in our little world had his own knee-padded choice firmly lined up for the job. As a result, only the hot favourite, a rank impossible outsider and myself were short listed and duly presented ourselves before the interviewing board.

To the great dismay of the pre-elected candidate, his patron was not present, having suddenly been taken ill. In his place sat an even more influential, lifelong opponent of his views and methods of patronage.

Somewhat dazed by the turn of events, I sat before the board listening to the substitute personality answering all the questions for me. I hardly spoke a word except to acquiesce and, after my inevitable appointment, I reflected rather ruefully that I had been elected by the selfsame system I despised and had spoken out against for many years. I had been flung upstairs by personal animosity towards the favourite's sponsor and not by any of my possible merits. Hardly a morale booster and not a world-shattering increase financially.

However, the Head laughed heartily and we worked together harmoniously for many years until his retirement. It was then that authority saw fit to leave open the Headmaster's post for a prolonged period and appointed me as Acting Headmaster, a position giving little satisfaction since one hung in limbo, tolerated but not accepted by the mighty and held in suspicion by the rank and file.

There was one advantage to all this, the opportunity to view the minor capers of educational life with a greater detachment than one can achieve in the classroom. This was just as well since, as always, events of a ludicrous rather than prestigious nature veered in my direction as towards a lodestone. The pigeon crisis, not any educational success, became the episode by which my brief period of glory was remembered.

Mr Wrayson first noticed the hidden riches aloft. He was a well educated, middle-aged man of unusually wide experience for a teacher, not given to hasty or immoderate speech but on this occasion the habits of a lifetime were abruptly modified.

A certain gentle pattering of small particles upon his bald head directed his gaze upwards to the trapdoor in the section of ceiling above his teaching desk. Of an inquiring turn of mind, he minutely examined the descending material with considerable interest.

His conclusions brought him with uncharacteristic haste to my office. He was normally very dignified and even a little pedantic so his succinct description of the offending matter in one four letter word convinced me of the urgency of the situation.

Following my request for immediate examination, the caretaker arrived bearing a ladder. He climbed up to the trapdoor from the edges of which the particles had escaped, investigated and confirmed Mr Wrayson's diagnosis. Indeed, he repeated the word several times most emphatically as his efforts to dislodge the trap caused further showers of the substance to descend upon his head and shoulders.

It took the combined efforts of three of us, perched precariously on the ladder, to force open the trap against the weight of the material upon it. It gave at last and the caretaker mounted higher to survey the loft. For several moments there was a very pregnant silence as he shone his torch around.

"Bloody hell!" he announced sepulchrally, "I don't believe it. It's like a nightmare up here!"

He descended and a marked aroma came down with him. I climbed up to look, along with Mr Wrayson. We viewed the loft space with incredulous awe. Even the reticent Wrayson called upon his Maker to bear witness to the sight.

Three feet deep in places, evidence of the productivity of our pigeons over the years beggared description. Joists were buried completely and all the supporting timbers so encrusted that they resembled gnarled branches or spurs of guano-whitened rock. The stench drove us down again and we closed the trap against the clinging wafts of ammonia. Effects of a possible ceiling collapse beneath the weight defied imagination.

It took repeated notifications before I could impress the gravity of our plight upon the building department but eventually they sent along a surveyor to see what this idiot Head was rabbiting on about. His reaction was well worth the wait. Clothes patchily whitened and smelling most offensively, he could not reach the telephone quickly enough.

He certainly galvanised normally lethargic departments by the urgency conveyed in his report. Half a dozen of the largest and heaviest men available were sent with shovels to push their big feet through our ceilings as they shovelled them clear. Huge waste disposal skips stood in the playground to receive their offerings.

Our whole atmosphere filled with a fog of floating particles. The floors became coated in grey dust and the entire surrounding area acquired a distinctly rural smell.

There were fringe benefits attached to the operation. We were avoided like the plague. No-one from officialdom wished to visit us no matter how urgent their business. Parents found that their children's' problems were no longer quite so pressing. Complaints needed to be genuine and very serious to be pursued through the aura that pervaded the school. Even our best friends avoided us at work, and outside too, until the clinging scent had blown from our persons. In splendid isolation, undisturbed save for the telephone, we taught in peace. It was, at times, almost worth the cleansing activities.

Only one unusually fussy parent was persistent enough to continue her disturbance of our labours. Each morning, without fail, she would ring and demand speech with the Acting Head about some trivial matter or another. No-one else would do. It had to be the Head in person. I suffered this daily until the morning of the fire.

I smelt the fire from afar off as I drove to school. The odour was most unpleasant and the nearer I approached the building the fouler it became. Billowing clouds of dense smoke filled the playground as I drove into it. The air was pungent with the fumes from burning ordure, feathers and the bodies of long dead pigeons. Our caretaker had utilised one of the partially filled skips to dump his still hot boiler ashes. The contents had ignited and the odour from the smouldering mass was staggering. It was tangible, palpable almost rather than a mere offence to the nasal organs.

Quickly organising a bucket chain of delighted pupils, we doused the malodorous fire and I was busily engaged in digging over the contents of the skip to ensure no spark remained when the fussy parent telephoned.

The school secretary, a frail, gentle lady of mature years, replied that the Head was not then available for consultation.

"Why can I not speak with him?" came the indignant response, "What is he doing that is so important he cannot listen to a parent?"

"You cannot speak with him, madam," blandly replied the secretary, "because he is at this moment busily shovelling manure."

The audible gasp from the telephone was the last our long suffering secretary heard of that particular parent for a very long time.

I have never been quite sure if "manure" was the word used by our demure but very resourceful secretary.

'Honi Soit ...'

A surfeit of school atmosphere and the great aura of upper working class respectability surrounding the job began to pall after I had been teaching for some long time. Not that the vast majority of teachers would ever admit to a working class status. Some quirk of mental gymnastics enables them to equate a labourer's wage level with middle class pretensions. Constant and very conscious emphasis on the highbrow nature of their leisure pursuits and the avoidance in conversation of all matters crude or 'not quite nice' began to induce in me a nostalgia for some of the vulgar pursuits of a long past army existence. In the parlance of this latter, the academic life was 'getting on my tits'.

At this stage, Harry Greatorex, whose earthy friendship provided a welcome contrast to my working ambience, persuaded me to accompany him to an evening of beer and entertainment by exotic dancers or, in other words, strippers.

Conditioned over the school years to regard this low type

entertainment as titillation for dirty-minded old men, I almost refused his invitation, thereby nearly denying myself an evening of innocent entertainment and a healthy purging of staff room prissiness. Not least of all I would have missed the pleasure of making the acquaintance of Gloria de l'Ange, alias Betty from the Co-op.

In anticipation of a shamefaced slinking into some obscure and disreputable building, I dressed to meet Harry in the seediest clothes of a far from elegant wardrobe and topped off the ensemble with a cloth cap. The cap had never been worn since Harry's aged and very frankly spoken mother had remarked of me: "I've seen worse looking chaps than you, Geoff, but you do look a bugger in that hat!"

Harry's remarks were equally outspoken when he saw me. "Where do you think we're going,then? A tramps' ball?"

The entrance to the show was brilliantly lit and a steady flow of well-dressed gentlemen entered in a manner that was anything but furtive. Our own entrance had a boisterous quality about it. Harry seemed to know everyone and the entire audience greeted him affably as we took our seats at a ringside table.

A true sense of priorities was established by a long preliminary period in which to drink beer and converse before the ceremonies commenced. At length, loud bouncing music shook the glasses on our table and the first exotic dancer bounded upon the stage.

Her extreme physical fitness became impressively apparent. No games mistress could ever have matched her strenuous gyrations. She pranced, she kicked, she bent and rolled in all directions to the thumping rhythm of the music. These vigorous calisthenics began in voluminous and highly improbable garments which she slowly and laboriously shed, rather like an energetic Eskimo preparing for bed.

The audience, extremely extrovert in nature, seemed to be singularly devoid of the dirty-minded old men reputed to make up such gatherings. Its main interest seemed to be in liquid refreshment and the poor girl attracted only such attention as could be given from over the rim of a glass. True, there was the occasional shout of encouragement.

"Get 'em off, love!"

"Come on down, lass! Me mate's short sighted!"

"Hurry up, gal. I want my glass filled."

One more sensuous wiggle and, amid a crescendo of sound, the last wisp fell away leaving her posed dramatically in her birthday suit. The room was cold and from our close vantage point we could see the goose pimples.

An unfortunate lull in the rowdy conversation coincided with Harry's casual observation. "What a hooter!" he remarked. The dancer directed a glance of pure venom towards him and her exit from the stage contained more indignation than erotic invitation. Certainly her nose was the most salient feature and the audience roared delightedly. It was its first sign of real emotion other than enthusiasm for beer.

A prolonged pause followed, designed unsuccessfully to work up lustful anticipation for the next act. When everyone had been liberally supplied with beer, the music thumped out again and the 'Gorgeous, Wonderful, Glamorous Gloria de l'Ange' was announced. In approximate time to the music, she pranced out before us.

Rhythmically, her more than ample charms hurtled in all directions. She spun, she swayed and then stopped dead in mid wiggle. Stock still, she stood looking down at Harry.

"Good Gawd!" said Gloria, "Are YOU here?"

"Hello love," responded Harry, "You've changed jobs then?"

She thudded and wobbled her way around again until, down to basics, she descended the steps from the stage and danced around our table.

"Mind your heads when I get this off," she warned us quietly, working hard to release her brassière. "There won't be room for you and me when I do!"

She was absolutely right. We ducked our heads to avoid sandbagging as she gyrated round the table and raised them with some relief as she leaped back on to the stage.

Her act concluded and her person re-clad, Gloria joined us for a drink.

"Meet Betty. Used to be in the local Co-op," Harry introduced her.

"The one near his shop," she amplified, "We're old mates."

Gloria, it transpired in conversation, was more than a little put out by her working conditions. Things were tough, she said. Her work in a neighbouring city had folded up altogether.

"Used to be dead easy," she confided. "I could walk from club to club in the evening and do the same act four or five times. Now I've got to travel around and run a car. More overheads and no time left for the old man and the kid. Spoiling me home life !"

We nodded sympathetically, unable to trust our speech.

"It's their dirty-minded Watch Committee," she went on. "Closed all the clubs. What they think goes on in a strip joint, I don't know!"

She summed up our evening's entertainment very accurately.

"More vice in a chapel vestry," she asserted.

A Lost Generation

*P*arents are frequently a great worry to their teenaged children. My son often complained of parental irresponsibility but never so loudly as he did following the purchase of his first motorcycle.

Since he was rising sixteen at this time, the spectre of his inevitable involvement in the perils of motorcycling had loomed largely in our thoughts for the last year or so. Obviously we could not selfishly deny him the horrific risks of teenage riding in order to preserve our own peace of mind. The urge would have to be worked out of his system, even though we knew we would develop ears like conch shells through listening for the engine beat of his safe return each night or the ominous knock on the door by a policeman bearing bad news.

Acting on the principle of concluding distasteful matters as early as possible, I had been secretly on the lookout for a cheap bike from my son's fifteenth birthday onwards.

With the cheerful assistance of my good friend Charlie Drinkwater, I finally located a suitable machine in a Bletchley scrapyard. It was a rusting non-runner, a B.S.A. C.10. 250cc, covered in atmospheric filth and cobwebs. There was no haggling. Five pounds changed hands and Chas and I pushed my purchase back to his house. It was no shining beauty but all the essential parts seemed to be present and I quite looked forward to helping my son with the restoration of the ancient bike.

There remained the problem of transporting the thing to our own town. Since it neither ran nor rejoiced in tax and insurance, it had to be carried. Charlie's caravan proved to be the solution. With great difficulty and many appeals to the Almighty, we manhandled it into the van, only to discover that it was impossible to anchor the thing down securely enough for it not to thrash the interior of the van to pieces.

Charlie Drinkwater resolved the problem but showed little regard for my physical wellbeing and future love life in the process. I was to mount the bike, grip the handle bars and, with both feet firmly on the floor, 'ride' it home. He closed the door on me with a sadistic grin and set off for the motorway.

Many of the M1 drivers overtaking us appeared more than a little alarmed to see a motorcycle apparently being ridden inside a caravan by a middle-aged maniac. Actually, my facial expressions reflected the effect of the van's brutal suspension system upon the more delicate areas of my anatomy and were wholly unrelated to their curious stares.

Jonathan's astonished delight at the arrival of the machine compensated a little for the crippled cowboy style of walking that afflicted me for several hours after the completion of my 'ride'. He was not so pleased when I finally started up the bike.

With the unbounded enthusiasm of youth he was all for painstakingly stripping it down to its individual components and reassembling it with loving care. "Not so," I told him. "Ancient machinery is like ageing folk. If either of them is in working order leave well alone and don't tamper with the mechanism."

In pursuance of this truism, we poured the necessary liquids into the appropriate orifices, charged up the battery and prepared for the moment of truth. It was not my fault that he chose to stand directly behind the bike, nor that the exhaust system was filled with soot, spiders' webs and insects various enough to interest an entomologist. Certainly I could not have foreseen or even hoped that the machine would start up at the first kick.

His unfilial comments, as he removed the assorted debris from his person, were pointed and extremely ungrateful, casting grave doubts upon the sense of responsibility of my generation. My howls of mirth did nothing to mollify him.

We re-tyred the bike and Jonathan lovingly scraped, sanded and painted till it shone respectably if not quite like new. Licensed and insured, it stood waiting to be ridden. Much to Jon's chagrin, I proposed to take it out for a test run. He still lacked a month to his sixteenth birthday and could do nothing about it.

I think frustration may have lent colour to his criticism of my riding clothes. An old fur coat, balaclava helmet, plastic pixie hood and wellington boots were perhaps not 'with-it' gear for the road but the weather was cold and my old motorcycling kit had long since gone,

The years fell away as I rode it round the streets. One circuit more and his mother joined me. Off we clattered, out towards the countryside, youth renewed and twenty years shrugged off. In a euphoric state we halted to fill up the petrol tank. The young pump attendant eyed our gear incredulously.

"Which grade?" he demanded, covertly examining us.

"I don't know. What do the things eat these days?" I replied.

He served us in haste, certain, I think, of our recent mechanised escape from restraint in some mental institution.

I opened the throttle and left him in a spray of wheel flung gravel as we settled down to enjoy our freshly restored youth. The ancient machine shuddered its way up to around fifty miles an hour as we approached the sharp bend round the village green.

At the crucial moment there came a certain lack of co-operation between rider and pillion passenger. I leaned stylishly into the corner and my better half, alarmed at the sudden deviation from the vertical, leaned hard out the other way. The more I leaned in to correct the balance, the more she leaned out. Our opposed efforts resulted in an unhappy compromise. We carried straight on, right across the green in fact, and spilled ourselves ignominiously at the other side.

A group of leather clad greasers, lounging by their beautiful high powered bikes, watched dispassionately as we picked up our machine and prepared to remount it and depart.

"And they have the bloody cheek to rabbit on about us!" commented one through his chewing gum.

"Bloody old tearaways!" sneered another.

We took to the road a little more soberly and headed homewards before worse befell us. Our son's indignation was reasonably restrained as he ruefully examined the scratches on his bike.

"Can't let you out of sight for two minutes together," he nagged, "You're neither of you fit to be loose on your own."

I let this pass. What really hurt was his refusal to let us ride his bike again. Just as we'd begun to enjoy it!

'Crabbed Age....'

*O*n the announcement to Jonathan of our impending retirement, during one of his rare visits to the ancestral bungalow,
an expression of anxiety bordering on apprehension abruptly displaced the look of indulgent tolerance he normally assumed
when listening to the oft repeated conversation of his ageing parents.

For a moment I was touched. The poor chap, I thought, was
worrying needlessly about our advancing age. I should have
known better.

"How on earth d'you think I shall keep track of you?" he
demanded. "It's only your jobs that hold you down!"

We thanked him for his filial concern but he did not hear us in
his agitation.

"Remember what happened during all the long holidays," he
complained. "I've been bailing you both out of trouble since I was
nine!"

He had attained this tender age when we decided to motor down through Spain to Tangier. This was many years before Spain achieved political enlightenment, good roads and a vast tourist trade. Prices were ridiculously low, tourists rare except along the northern coast, and the regime was inflexible.

Clattering our way over the then apology for a highway to Madrid, we entered the city during the rush hour. Tired and hungry after much abortive searching for a suitable hotel, I pulled in alongside a traffic cop and sought his advice. With no softening of his glare of authority, he opened the car door, courteously beckoned Joan to change to a back seat and took her place alongside me. He indicated that I should start the engine and waved me forward. Somewhat puzzled, I let in the clutch and followed his directions, uncertain as to whether we had broken some mysterious fascist regulation and were on our way to officialdom or being guided to an hotel.

Hailing from a land of benign 'bobbies', I marvelled at the manner in which the hitherto merciless traffic stood on its brakes to give way to us when they spotted the law in my passenger's seat. Following 'Dead-pan's' gestured directions, I left the main roads to twist and turn down ever narrowing and seedy looking side streets until we drew up outside a small doorway bearing the notice 'Hotel Miranda'.

Taking our passports, the policeman led us to the reception desk, brusquely displaced two or three people in process of booking in, slapped the passports on the desk, pocketed the notes slipped across the desk by the receptionist, held out his other hand at thigh level for my contribution to the one-man police charity and departed.

Ushered upstairs through an establishment innocent of any dining room, lounge or other communal areas, we were shown not into a bedroom but a very ornate suite. There was a main bedroom, a dressing room with a bed in it for Jon and the most magnificent marble bathroom I had ever seen.

Stunned by the opulence of it all, we took a moment or two to fully appreciate the decor. Voluptuous nudes disported themselves on two of the bedroom walls and a ceiling to floor mirror almost covered the third wall. The fourth only had a conventional decoration in white and gold. We lay on the bed, laughing at the mild erotica on the ceiling, when Jon's voice summoned us to his small room.

"Look at my pictures, Dad! They're as big as me and all starkers!"

The penny dropped. A year had elapsed since the Spanish government had closed all the state owned brothels. Thriftily, the better appointed ones had been converted to hotels. Ours had obviously been a luxury job.

The staff appeared to be as unorthodox as the establishment itself. In the process of changing, I stood clad in an aertex vest, trousers and underwear round my ankles when the chambermaid entered unannounced to turn down the beds. She stood for a moment critically appraising my various attributes before raising two fingers in what I hoped was a signal to pull up my pants and proceeding to adjust the sheets. As Joan later suggested, perhaps the hotel conversion included the original staff as well as the building.

Arriving eventually in Tangier, we joined with two American ladies in hiring an Arab guide to show us the sights. Punctilious, despite a somewhat elastic knowledge of the English language, he indicated any detail likely to be of interest, pointing out to the ladies the house of the American Consul. Since this gem of information came out as "The Yankee Basha live here", the two Americans engaged in bewildered speculation as to whether it was the holiday residence of Joe Louis. I explained to them and we continued to the Pillars of Hercules. Our guide, obviously fearful of poaching, handed us over temporarily to the resident custodian of the caves.

This comedian posed dramatically against the entrance, quoted the aperture and speed setting for photography in that light and held out his hand for baksheesh. Greatly taken aback by tourists without a camera, he demanded a cigarette.

Gently explaining that I did not smoke, I added for good measure: "Anna englesi moskeen."

This protestation of poverty obviously touched him for he produced a heavy silver cigarette case and offered me one of his.

Our own voluble guide parted from us at midday after guiding us to the restaurant of his choice and graciously accepting financial tribute from the proprietor and ourselves.

We ate well and emerged, blinking a little, into the dazzling streets, deserted during siesta time except for the shoe-shine youths squatting somnolently against the wall. The Americans sauntered past them, a little distance ahead of us. One of the youths opened his eyes, nudged his mate and made a suggestion regarding the two ladies that was reminiscent of my Cairo days. Casting Arabic insults at foreign tourists was evidently a regular sport during the siesta time scarcity of policemen. I awaited our turn.

The lad opened his mouth as we drew abreast and, forgetting I was no longer a soldier and had a family with me, I beat him to it, describing his incestuous relationships and his immediate predecessors in the gutter Arabic of the Cairo slums. His jaw fell and we were some yards past before he sufficiently recovered from the surprise to shout a short commentary on my sexual habits.

"Ya'alla, zifti yehudi kelb!"

The ultimate insult sprang to my lips before I remembered my present status and the absence of a .38 Smith and Wesson.

Our previous exchange of personal pleasantries had been mere badinage, but to call an Arab a filthy dog and a Jewish one at that would have brought out the knives in Cairo. There was an ominous silence behind us and I hastened our pace a little until we were able to turn into a cafe and order drinks.

I lingered over mine long after the other two had finished. Over the other side of the road, my shoe-shine youths had assembled with four or five reinforcements. They all talked animatedly and from time to time the most voluble, my verbal adversary's pal, gesticulated towards the cafe.

When it became impossible to further prolong our stay, I hurried us along towards the city centre. The gang matched us step for step on the opposite pavement. Wishing heartily for the appearance of a policeman in the deserted street, I watched the youths converge upon us as we paused at the crossroads. Grinning delightedly, they surrounded us. The one who had been pointing us out at the cafe seized Jon's hand, shook it vigorously and pronounced in high glee: "Your Fader spik Arab good. Make big fool of Abdul. All laugh big.'"

Abdul smiled sheepishly and shook my hand. I breathed again, the villainous crowd rolled about in mirth and Abdul joined in.

After this shattering anticlimax, the return journey northwards passed in a pleasantly uneventful manner until we drove into Irun, preparatory to crossing the frontier into France.

It was my fault that we almost missed our way in the town. It was signed clearly enough. Since we were travelling very slowly looking for the sign I had just missed, I made a very sharp turn at the deserted crossroads and the tyres squealed slightly.

From nowhere, it seemed, a policeman leaped into our path, hand upraised.

He leaned in through the open window, filled the car with garlic laden breath, scowled fiercely and pointed dramatically at a point on the speedometer which the most optimistic manufacturer would never claim the car could achieve, even on the open road with a following tail wind.

Modestly I disclaimed such sporting performance but this only evoked a spate of staccato shouting and arm waving that implied our entry into the town had all but broken the sound barrier. A little sharper, this time, I denied the possibility of such a dramatic arrival. The cop's scowl and complexion deepened. Producing a tattered wallet, he rubbed thumb and forefinger together in unmistakable demands for a bribe. Nourished in Britain on the legend of police incorruptibility and correspondingly outraged by this demand, I requested him to remove his presence in very basic English and equally explicit French.

I had forgotten the regime he served and from his furious reaction we gathered that he had more than a smattering of French. Snatching the passport from my grasp he ordered me to accompany him to headquarters. My reception was by no means cordial. A French-speaking gentleman seated at a vast polished desk leafed through my passport. He paused at a page containing entry and exit stamps from our passage through Gibraltar and addressed me loudly and abusively on the evils of British possession of the Rock. It seemed that Britain was the most perfidious usurper in the whole of Europe and that I was a typical example of her decadence and probably personally responsible for much of it.

A little incensed by the injustice of all this, I thoughtlessly countered with a brief, anatomically biased, remark on what he could do with his own country's regime. The chain reaction to this was spectacular. Every jack-in-office in the place sprang to his feet raised his arm aggressively and heaped abuse upon me. A couple of guardia seized me by the arms, hustled me through a door, down a flight of stone steps, into a square chamber lined with battered cell doors. One of these was unlocked, I was propelled inside and the key turned on me.

Considerably taken aback by the turn of events, I sat on the stone sleeping bench and weighed up the situation.

Light came into the rough stone cell from a narrow horizontal slit at ceiling height. Standing up on the bench, I could see through the bars that this was at ground level outside. I was housed in what would have made a very good film set for a mediaeval prison scene. Previous occupants had left their names scratched into the dirty whitewash of the walls. All were Spanish except one, Harry Bishop. Adding my name to the list, I pondered on the folly of reacting to provocation and what course of action I should take.

At length, naively believing in the rights of foreigners to contact their national representatives even in a fascist regime, I booted the cell door and told the scruffy minion who appeared that I needed to see someone in authority. Almost immediately the desk-bound interrogator appeared and brusquely demanded what all the row was about. My request to see the British Consul met with derisive mirth and a suggestion regarding that gentleman that I am sure he would not have welcomed.

Non-plussed by this refusal, I lowered my sights to a very modest request for my jacket which was in the car. Surprisingly, he acquiesced to this and departed. By some quirk of regulations or perhaps a good knowledge of his own personnel, he had the jacket brought down to me by Jonathan, escorted by a guardia.

Possible accusations of pilfering from the pockets, en route, had been avoided. My wife had not been asked to bring the jacket since, in the strait-laced Spain of that era, she had no chaperone and might have brought embarrassing accusations of her own.

Jon seemed more amused than alarmed by my incarceration

and, as I took the coat from him, I told him in very rapid English to tell his mother to contact the British Consul in San Sebastian.

She did better than this. Informing the senior official of her intentions, she started the car to drive to the consulate and was about to move off when he hastily asked her to wait a moment. The matter could be settled, perhaps, if he contacted Madrid.

Within an hour I was taken upstairs and details copied from my passport into an impressive looking folder before it was handed back to me. I must not, it was emphasised, attempt to leave Spain until the affair was concluded. Where was I staying that night? At random I picked on Burgos. On arrival, I was told, I must report to the Burgos police.

This was repeated to me as I started the car and headed for the Burgos road.

Out of sight, we doubled back straight for the frontier, joined the short tourist queue and drove out into France. They were perhaps still waiting for me at Burgos when the British Foreign Office complained about the incident.

Years later, quoting this Irun episode as a reason for great anxiety about what he considered to be a potential rake's progress through early retirement, our son disclaimed all moral responsibility for our future actions abroad and in GB.

"Don't worry, lad," we reassured him. "We're no longer incident prone. We're getting old now."

"Hand me the maps," said Joan as Jonathan and his wife went to bed. "We'll need to do something special for a last fling!"

ONLY FOOLS DRINK WATER

Written by GEOFFFREY MORRIS and illustrated by PATRICIA KELSALL

"...We sat down for lunch after a hot and strenuous morning gathering in the straw. I was distressingly dehydrated. Pitchers of water stood ready to dilute the *pastis* to individual taste. The temptation was too great for me. I reached for a water jug and filled an empty glass to the brim. It had barely touched my parched lips when cries of consternation and incredulity came from all sides.

"That's water! WATER, I tell you!"

"You'll derange yourself!"

"Don't you know the harm straight water can do?"

"You can't drink it like that!"

"You've put it in the wrong glass. There's your pastis!"

There was even a serious appeal from one of the helpers who thought that I spoke no French.

"Do something! Stop him! He'll do himself a mischief! These *sacré* foreigners have no idea how to look after their health!"

It was as though I had brought out a hip flask of whisky at a total abstainers' convention..."

The author and his wife – jokingly dubbed "senile delinquents" by their long-suffering son – have been enjoying hilarious escapades in the Charente-Maritime marshlands of France for more than 40 years. They have lived there for 20 years and are now naturalised French. This delightful book describes their experiences.

ISBN 1 901253 10 4   Price £8.99

Order from your bookshop – or direct from the publisher, Leonie Press, 13 Vale Rd, Hartford, Northwich, Cheshire, CW8 1PL (adding £1.30 for post and packing)